TEAM LEADERSHIP

D1483668

HOW TO ORDER THIS BOOK

TEAM
LEADERSHIP

School Boards
at Work

MICHAL K. ROSENBERGER, Ph.D.

TECHNOMIC
PUBLISHING CO., INC.
LANCASTER · BASEL

Team Leadership

a **TECHNOMIC**®publication

Published in the Western Hemisphere by
Technomic Publishing Company, Inc.
851 New Holland Avenue, Box 3535
Lancaster, Pennsylvania 17604 U.S.A.

Distributed in the Rest of the World by
Technomic Publishing AG
Missionsstrasse 44
CH-4055 Basel, Switzerland

Printed in the United States of America
10 9 8 7 6 5 4 3 2

Main entry under title:
   Team Leadership: School Boards at Work

A Technomic Publishing Company book
Bibliography: p. 157
Includes index p. 163

Library of Congress Catalog Card No. 96-62020
ISBN No. 1-56676-526-9

To those high-performing leadership teams that overcome the challenges to provide quality education for all their students, and to those that are striving to be!

CONTENTS

INTRODUCTION

WHEN I tell people that I spend my evenings at meetings of local school boards and that I'm writing this book, I receive amused laughter, surprised looks, and expressions of disbelief. Why write a book about school boards? What is so compelling about school boards that I would want to research their role, attempt to define it more clearly, and seek the reasons for their low status in many of our communities?

The short answer is, I believe, that school boards are our (only?) hope for school reform. I believe trustees are well meaning individuals who care about kids. With John Carver and Robert Greenleaf, I believe they can make a difference as "servant-leaders" when they are provided the tools to govern schools. The longer answer? Well . . .

For ten years as a teacher and school counselor, I noticed that most schools were not healthy workplaces for anyone. Like a building inspector in a fine-looking building, I first noticed hairline cracks, then structural flaws; I wanted to know what could be done to repair the damages. So, off I went to The University of Texas to study school improvement.

In Austin I studied organizational behavior, educational leadership and politics, consultation skills, adult education, and ethical behavior. Trying to settle on a dissertation topic, I researched "School Restructuring," "Team Leadership," "Group Dynamics," and "Developing Efficacy through Training." Then, when I found *no* correlation between the job description, training, and what school counselors actually *do,* I was ready to study the complex world of school boards!

All that research became background information when I was hired to write a curriculum for school trustees. Because, like most citizens, I had little knowledge about what members of the local school board need to know and be able to do (the basis for a curriculum), I researched the role. But the more I searched, the more I found it a closed "black box."

> When engineers draw a diagram of a complicated machine, they use a sort of shorthand. Instead of drawing all the details, they put a box to stand for a whole bunch of parts and label the box with what that bunch of parts is supposed to do. So a "black box" is a label for what a bunch of things are supposed to do.
>
> Bateson

First I visited with the directors of the many departments in the association. The Texas Association of School Boards (TASB) has a large and talented staff, providing resources and technical suport for Texas school trustees in the areas of school law, personnel, training, policy development, risk management, and strategic planning. Each department had a piece of the information I needed. Curiously, though, they didn't seem to share information with each other. I was reminded of the ancient tale of the blind men describing an elephant. One described a tail, another the leg, and so forth. Each believed he had the whole picture, when he had only one part!

Even publications provided little illumination through the fog. I went first to the bulletins and journals provided by the state school board associations. I found that although the material was cloaked in different formats, the content was markedly similar, providing a general view of responsibilities, but few concrete suggestions. Most literature describes overall responsibilities, such as policymaking and goal setting.

Dissertations define some of the challenges of delineating the role, but few describe effective governance. There are, however, countless demographic studies that describe the characteristics of board members. Although knowing ages and ethnicity of trustees was interesting, I couldn't see how it would improve the quality of governance.

I reread books on school improvement and restructuring and was dismayed that boards are usually left out of the information loop. Few research-oriented journals feature articles regarding school board issues, effective governance, or the interdependence of good governance and systemic school reform. The few books and journals on school governance led me back to other publications regarding team leadership, corporate governing bodies, and the political milieu of education.

I went to workshops and conferences with novice trustees, seeking practical information on educational governance. We found their role poorly defined, even misrepresented. The training was so shallow that I had the impression that *anyone* could quickly become an effective trustee. The complexities of school politics, the leadership functions of the local board, and their role in school improvement are seldom discussed. The role was described in a passive way. Workshops, seminars, and conferences provided disconnected pieces but no overall structure. Nowhere was the research on the complexities and paradoxes of groups or strategies for effective team leadership discussed.

When I asked superintendents to share materials and anecdotes about their boards, they sent me sample agendas and board packets. The items on the agendas had little connection to the content of the training I had attended: "Review and Approval of Checks," "Bids on Food Services, Products, and Supplies," "Carpet Replacement," "Proposed Ground Lease for Radio Tower, Bowie High School." The chasm between the stated role and responsibilities and how boards spend their meeting time was amazing!

Eventually I stumbled over Carver's *Boards That Make a Difference,* Schlechty's *Schools for the 21st Century,* Institution for Educational Leadership's *School Boards; Strengthening Grassroots Leadership,* and Lutz and Merz's *School/Community Relations. Finally,* I had models of effective governance, assurances that boards were important in school improvement, and acknowledgement of the political context of education. I highly recommend the quartet to all persons interested in governance issues.

Then, I visited with trustees about their role, how they learned it, and what they *wished* they had learned. Individual trustees would tell me that they became a member of the local board in order to make a difference for kids: "I was passionate about doing my part to save the schools." I have found trustees to be, usually, well-intentioned folk, but their board meetings are boring and focused on budgets and buildings. Newspapers are full of board nonsense: expelling students because of hair length, switching off microphones, and canceling student programs.

I tried to determine why there is such disparity between the expressed beliefs of individual trustees and the actual performance of boards. Is there a mismatch between the complexity of school systems and the abilities of the board members? Are current trustees less capable of leadership than former ones? I wondered, as others had before me, why these committed citizens fail to develop into high-performance teams. Perhaps if I could learn why it is so difficult to work as a board, I could learn why effective boards are so rare.

Because all my research and interviews failed to yield a clear role description, eventually I developed a coalition of experts within TASB to agree on the knowledge, skills, and attitudes ("ksa's") essential for an effective trustee. Although I was unhappy when the seventeen-page listing described the role as a passive one, at last I had confirmation that the role was more extensive than described. This list was the basis for the *beginning* of a comprehensive board development curriculum: an eight-hour orientation. The interactive training combined key issues from the list with research on school improvement, leadership skills, and the team development process.

Questions continued to emerge about school governance. The more I learned, the more confused I was. For example, the seventeen-page listing of knowledge, skills, and attitudes described a very passive and reactive role that *discouraged* any leadership role on the part of the school board. I continued to find personal, social, political, and structural barriers that obstruct leadership, but few wanted to discuss them.

Finally, the answer to the black box problem emerged: training, literature, and board agendas are *meant* to impede effective governance, sometimes by default, sometimes on purpose! In an article by university professors in the October 1993 issue of *Educational Leadership* I saw, in print, encouragement for superintendents to *disable school boards.* The authors, Professors Heller and Rancic, urge superintendents to manage their boards by *burying them with information* and *overloading agendas with trivia!*

Elected citizens believe they are joining a real board; instead they usually find they have joined a façade, a "nominal board" that serves only to satisfy the legal requirement and provide the cover of legitimacy (Greenleaf). Even the authority of the board over the superintendent becomes blurred. Although the board hires the superintendent, trustees are socialized to accept the chief school administrator's definitions of situations and behave as though *they* work for the *superintendent*, instead of the other way around.

When the eager novices attend meetings, they find the agenda burdened with "administrivia" concerning milk bids or a computer for the junior high or the placement of a radio tower. None of these are policy decisions; they are administrative responsibilities placed on agendas to fill time. But, because of peer pressure and the socialization process, trustees collude with the agenda-maker and spend time on things that either do not need to be done or are a waste of time for them to do. Such collusion takes a serious toll on the integrity and sense of efficacy of well-meaning citizens.

Elected citizens are impeded in their real work of governing schools when superintendents feel there is no incentive to support boards to become skillful and pro-active. Many school leaders feel that the black box is like Pandora's: better kept closed than opened to unknowns. When board agendas focus on "administrivia," not policies, programs, and accountability, the superintendent is free to carry out his or her personal agenda.

Confused and frustrated by the rigid structure, trustees lose their sense of purpose and their ability to assert their power wisely. "Because power is not achieved in constructive ways, they turn to its destructive forms, so that at least they make some sort of difference" (Cell, 1984). When boards are derailed, micromanaging and fighting against each other, they are eliminated from important decisions, fail to govern, and public education suffers.

Education is, by its very nature, incestuous. But when retired or fired superintendents run the national and state school board associations, how zealous should we expect them to be in encouraging boards to assert their authority over their peers?

During this extensive research I wondered how lay persons would learn the true role of the local school board. If, as an educator for fifteen years, my knowledge of what trustees *really* did was severely limited, how do those with no connection to schools, except for their children, begin to know the complexities of our educational system? How would elected trustees learn the knowledge and skills to provide effective governance?

It is because of this lack of useful information for citizens, legislators, educators, and trustees that this book came to be written. This book doesn't attempt to provide all the answers, not even all the questions. But, hopefully it will provide useful information for *all* the stakeholders of our educational system. We must continually remember that schools do not belong to the educators, or even the parents. They belong to all the citizens!

By identifying and describing barriers to effective performance of local school boards, all of us can identify ways we can work together to improve school governance. I believe the future of public education for all our children is worth the effort!

CHAPTER 1

Challenges to Educational Governance

"To rule is easy," said Goethe, "to govern, difficult."

CURRENT PERCEPTION OF LOCAL GOVERNANCE

IT is difficult to overestimate the importance of local school governance. In the United States, 97,000 trustees on 15,350 boards exercise authority over a $300 billion industry and make decisions that determine the future of public education in America. School boards everywhere are the chief and, when the state permits it, supreme educational authority for the community. Within any given community, the board may be the biggest employer, serve the greatest number of "customers," and disperse more tax dollars than any other public agency.

The challenges to effective governance are also great! Whether elected or appointed, the policymakers are buffeted by constituents, tightly regulated by state authorities, and preside in the public spotlight over two emotional topics: children and money! They are expected to meet the educational needs of an increasingly diverse body of students with dwindling resources. They attempt to balance conflicting demands from diverse constituencies in a highly political arena threatened with taxpayer suit, popular referendum, and recall. Time and energy are dissipated by teacher union negotiations, paring the budget (again), and implementing expensive state mandates. Although boards have the potential to become leaders in school reform, the gap between what *is* and what *could be* has resulted in widespread disappointment. Instead of innovators, local school boards are perceived as barriers to school reform. Their performance is uneven and sometimes contentious, especially in urban communities. There are many of us who agree with Carver that "the system is mired in trivia, wasteful of its executive leadership and unable to find a handle on what, in fact to lead about" (Carver, 1991, p. 6).

Yet, in my work as consultant to boards and superintendents, trustees tell me that they became a member of the local board in order to "make a difference for kids." When they speak of their love of children and concern about children at risk, I believe them. *"I care about the kids. I don't know a lot about budget, but I care about the kids."*

Why, then, don't trustees use their governance powers to improve the quality of education? If trustees come to the board table with dreams, why don't they spend their time exploring, debating, and defining these dreams? My curiosity about why these committed citizens failed to develop into high-performance teams led me to extensive research, dozens of interviews, and countless board meetings. I wanted to know what happens between the campaign trail and the board room.

I found many reasons why committed and competent policymakers spend more time "minding the store" than developing and leading the educational program. Personal agendas, idiosyncrasies, and self-serving behaviors are relatively easy to identify and usually targeted as the primary problem. However, I found that effective performance is hindered by personal, social, organizational, and political factors that are rarely discussed.

PERSONAL CHALLENGES

Challenges to effective boardsmanship come even prior to election. Candidates usually are elected in a political process, competing with incumbents, unknowingly committing themselves to actions that are beyond the board's jurisdiction. When elected, they must become part of the existing governance team, often with persons they denigrated during the campaign. (If they campaigned against the superintendent, things become even more tense!) In addition, their constituency may expect instant pay-off of campaign promises, unaware that the trustee has no individual power.

Novice trustees are overwhelmed by the extensive time and information requirements. They do not anticipate the many demands on their time or the changes in their personal relationships. Leisure and family time disappear; some members spend up to thirty to forty hours a week in board-related activities. Reading and reviewing proposals, recommendations, and publications require at least as much time as formal meetings.

Especially for the novice trustee, there is either too much or too little information. Without *enough* information, a wise decision is impossible; with *too much* information, the trustee may become overwhelmed and acquiesce to the recommendation of the superintendent, conventional wisdom, and/or public pressure.

SOCIAL CHALLENGES

The social milieu structure creates its own challenges: board meetings provide textbook examples of group dynamics at work. Trustees have no individual power; they only can act as a group, yet there is little training for trustees regarding the advantages of team leadership, the dynamics of group development, the paradoxes of group life, or characteristics of effective groups.

Individuals can take advantage of their collective wisdom only when they have developed a collegial relationship with all other trustees, no matter how diverse their goals and agendas. But becoming a cohesive team in their fishbowl environment is almost impossible. Boards must have the opportunity for thoughtful deliberation and dialogue out of the public eye to develop trust, but in most states, they are constrained by "sunshine laws."

ORGANIZATIONAL CHALLENGES

> Where opportunity for leadership is greatest, job design is poorest!
>
> Houle

The role of the school trustee is complex, ambiguous, and political, but it comes with a simple, almost naive, job description. Like the proverbial glacier, the true role of the local school board is largely invisible; but unlike a glacier, it is fluid, changing with each new legislature. Although most candidates believe they *already* know everything (from what they read in the sensational (often negative) press and their ever-rising tax bill), at their first meeting they are overwhelmed. As one trustee said, "I felt as though I had been run over by a freight train."

Reconciling a simplified description of their role and responsibilities with their complex tasks and duties is frustrating:

> We all start out with one agenda that is the basis for running for the board in the first place. I think what sometimes you're forced to do, because of morass of bureaucratic uncertainty, you're forced to change your tactics in pursuit of your objectives.

Each trustee must become a financial whiz, building contractor, diplomat, and media and public relations expert, all in *public*! Although such a complex role requires diverse skills and expertise, there are no role requirements (except residency), and most trustees must learn this ambiguous and political role with little assistance. It takes 3–4 years to be effective, but most members leave after their first term.

Creating change requires stability, yet we would have a difficult time finding a more fluid body than the leadership team. The members of a school board are in a constant state of transition, with one-third of the members up for election in any given year. Superintendents rotate from district to district about every three years. When individuals leave, they remove knowledge from the pool of information; each new person deflects the energies and attention of the others, as incumbents bring them up to speed.

Because individual trustees have no authority outside of legally constituted board meetings, they must place their issues on an already burdened agenda. Instead of carrying out the goals they promised their constituents, trustees quickly find themselves overwhelmed with "administrivia." When trustees lack a clear understanding of their role in school governance *and* face an activity-based school board agenda, the descent into micro-management is a quick slide.

In addition, conferences for school trustees are more about maintaining the status quo than learning how to support systemic school reform with good governance. This is a serious omission, providing trustees "no reason to believe that our educational system is not humming along just fine. Here we have the elected leaders who alone can legally sanction reform at the local level and they are being educated in the routines of keeping the present system running efficiently" (Gibboney, 1991, p. 683).

POLITICAL CHALLENGES

In what was formerly a low-profile, low-conflict position, school boards have been thrust into the middle of today's turbulent political environment. They are the extension of social and political processes at the local, county, state, national, and international level. Districts bordering Mexico, for example, are required to use local resources (i.e., local taxes) to meet the extensive educational and social needs of immigrants from Central America.

Boards serve in a difficult situation, performing under rigorous local scrutiny, attempting to meet local needs within state and federal guidelines. The elected trustee must represent the constituency, yet these constituencies do not speak with one voice. Although the demands and expense of education are increasing, only 20 percent of the electorate have school children, causing many citizens to believe that they have no direct stake in the quality of education.

Pervasive apathy about schools and the citizens who govern them leads to elections where trustees are elected by as few as sixteen votes. One example of voter apathy took place in our nation's capital in 1994. District schools in Washington, D.C. opened late because of thousands of fire code violations. Student performance had not improved above their already abysmal levels and incumbents almost took a pay raise during the city's escalating fiscal crisis. Yet a majority of voters *failed to vote* in the school board races.

IMPROVING THE SYSTEM

Effective boards are clear about their role and receive support from the superintendent, staff, and community. They build bridges and coalitions to unite diverse stakeholders in attacks on shared problems. As true servant-leaders, they know how to couple the delegation of power with accountability.

The reasons for ineffective school board performance are as complex and interdependent as the role, but I believe local school boards can overcome all the obstacles with improved skills, support, and improved relationships. Because errors in performance most often result from flawed systems, not individuals, we must improve the *system* to improve the quality of governance.

Readers who wish to learn what school boards do and how they work (and why they don't) can create conditions for individual trustees and local school boards to provide better leadership for the educational community. We can restore effective governance to public education, but we must work together to overcome the barriers. We must insist that boards use their governing powers to make a difference in our educational system.

- *Legislators* must make education a priority and stabilize the funding process. Creating legislation at the state or national level, no matter how worthy, that must be funded at the local level creates conflict between the trustees and the community. They must rescind state-mandated micro-management. When laws force boards to focus on the "deck chairs," the trustees have no time to decide where the ship is going, much less steer it!

- *Candidates* must decide whether they are willing to commit the time and energy necessary for team leadership. They must be willing to become individually competent and join with others to become an informed and skillful political body.
- *Citizens* must select candidates who have the capacity, integrity, and wisdom to perform well in this high-pressure position. The electorate must understand the importance of electing persons who have the qualities and capacity for effective performance in the role; it is not a role for the overbusy or under-committed.
- *Business and industry* must encourage capable candidates, providing time off from duties when necessary.
- *Current boards and superintendents* must redesign their roles, continue their self-evaluation, and improve their working relationships.
- *Professors and students of educational leadership* must provide the tools to address the political context of educational governance and support collegial relationships between the superintendent and boards.

Because, in theory, local school governance represents participatory government, we *all* are responsible for the success of four local governing bodies. When we understand, eliminate, minimize, or manage the challenges and constraints inherent in the *system,* we can become part of the solution, not the problem. Collectively, we can devise ways to manage the personal, social, organizational, and political challenges so boards can ensure effective team leadership is provided to serve the community and its children.

This book will explore the current state of board governance and identify challenges and describe opportunities to overcome them. My wish is that citizens, educators, and board members will see the role of the board in a new way, breaking out of their old paradigms. I believe it is only when this information is understood by the general public that we will again elevate board membership to a position of status and authority. Educating the electorate about the qualities of an effective board member, the complex role of the board, and its importance might encourage the public to become more involved in school board member campaigns and elections.

First we will look at the problem within its political context. Personal and social challenges will be addressed in Chapters 3 through 5. Chapter 6 discusses strategies for harmonious relationships. Chapters 7 through 9 discuss meeting management and governance tools: policies, budget, and long-range planning. Chapter 10 provides the socio-political context for boards to become advocates for educational reform. Chapter 11 brings together suggestions for "growing" better boards.

If we agree with Phillip Schlechty (1990, p. 12) that "only boards . . . have the moral and legal authority to assert what kinds of knowledge should be taught in our schools," shouldn't they be the most knowledgeable, skillful, and committed governing boards in every community?

CHAPTER 2

The Political Context of School Governance

The conventional picture of how a board should function is founded in tradition, enforced by regulations of the Department of Education, promoted by the National School Boards Association [and the state associations] and expected by the [state] Legislature[s].

Carver, 1991

HISTORICAL BACKGROUND

AMERICANS are proud of their democratic governance of the public schools, and the local board is the heart of this education system. Selecting citizens to be trustees traces back to the New England colonies, when special committees were selected to provide for educational governance of the local school districts. Originally, these committees had complete and total control: they levied and collected taxes, hired and supervised teachers, provided school buildings, examined pupils and teachers, and certified progress. As the responsibilities grew, the need for special attention became evident and boards began to appoint superintendents in the 1830s. Local boards of education and superintendents have been defining (and re-defining) their respective roles ever since.

Local school boards are agents of the state, governed by state law. They are the supreme educational authority for the community within the parameters of state and federal laws, rules, mandates, and resources.

Members of the local school board are "trustees" for the public good, charged with the oversight of public schools. They are responsible for ensuring that schools are run in an efficient and effective manner and meet the appropriate state and federal standards. Trustees translate community needs, values, and expectations into policies, plans, and goals; in a parallel role, they interpret the policies of the school system to the community.

FEDERAL SUPPORT AND CONSTRAINTS

The authority for a public education system is granted by the federal government by the Tenth Amendment: "The powers not delegated to the United States by the Constitution, nor prohibited by it to the States, are reserved to the States."

Although by default the Constitution allows for state control of education, this "local control" is modified and constrained by statutory provisions, court decisions, and attorney generals' opinions. Federal funds also come with rules and regulations regarding their use and disbursement. National vs. local control is also modified by such paradoxical interventions as national curriculum standards and site-based decision making.

Courts have modified the governance of public schools through litigation at all levels. The Supreme Court has strongly influenced education through interpretations of the Fourteenth Amendment, guaranteeing equal opportunity to all children. Handicapped, bilingual, or poor cannot be deprived of an equal education due to a shortage of financial revenue. As legislatures wrestle with funding, the issue regularly returns to, and is judged by, the courts.

The political nature of education is further exemplified by the current discussion of disbanding the Department of Education, created in 1979. It is possible that, in the future, the Departments of Labor and Commerce may have more influence on our educational system because of the increasing demands from industry regarding student preparation.

STATE AND LOCAL INFLUENCES

State legislatures' influence over local educational policy has expanded as local districts providing growing academic demands are perceived as inadequate. In addition to laws regarding school funding and curriculum, there are sanctions for inadequate student performance or inefficient management of districts and campuses. Many states have instituted a statewide accountability system to compare student performance, staffing, and fiscal appropriations across districts.

At the state, regional, and local levels, school governance is arranged into semi-autonomous units and managed by elected and appointed officials and employees. All states have an education

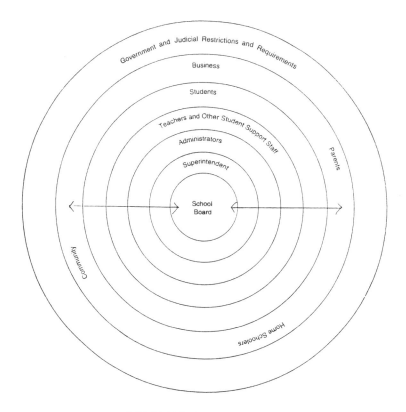

CIRCLES OF INFLUENCE

agency and state board of education that carries out the work of the legislature through an elected or appointed education commissioner.

The continually evolving role of the state education agency includes allocating and monitoring human and financial resources to local districts. Agency staff provide technical assistance to improve the effectiveness of schools, teachers, and administrators through staff and curriculum development. They may conduct educational research, develop and administer student and teacher testing programs, and provide information for policy development at the local or state level. They also monitor the training and performance of the governing bodies of the local districts. The policies set forth at the state level are then implemented by school administrators and staff locally, under the local school board.

Although the state mandates the curriculum and decides education policy, the board sets the tone for educational standards. Its hiring and budget decisions dictate the educational philosophy the district will follow. The school board hires the superintendent and delegates responsibility for most of the administrative functions. Although the superintendent usually initiates proposals for budget, policies, and personnel, final decisions are the board's responsibility.

Most boards have responsibilities regarding:

- district policy
- recruiting, hiring, and evaluating the superintendent of schools
- planning and goal setting
- financial resources
- school facilities
- instruction
- public relations
- adjudication and investigations
- retaining an attorney or law firm
- setting strategy and coordinating litigation efforts
- working with various officials and agencies

Local school boards receive their power and authority from the state, and each state has its own requirements and mandates. They must carry out state law: their lines of legal responsibility go directly to the state. At the same time, all school boards generate "laws" of their own. That is, they establish policies for governing schools.

PORTRAITS OF SCHOOL DISTRICTS AND THEIR BOARDS

Every local board has its own culture, operating style, and norms. Its behavior reflects local tradition, values, education, and wealth. The local social and political scene is reflected in the attitude of the public and their expectations of the board. Behavior and relationships are also influenced by the capacity and skill of the superintendent and board president.

The geography and setting of the administration building provide the context for the board's performance. Board meetings in small communities are far removed by distance and spirit from the policymaking and rule-setting (and sometimes contentious) governing bodies in the city. On-site visits are helpful in understanding the context of board behavior and practice. Consider the similarities and differences of these settings.

Small Urban District

Nestled right off the town circle, the former high school now housed the administrative offices and the board room. It was a classic brick building with steep stairs to the entrance. Two tall boys dressed in blue jeans and windbreakers came out and sat side by side on the top step. I joked with them about not being able to stay away from school as we went in, and they responded good-naturedly.

We took our time on the way in, admiring the restored building. Black and white photos dating back to the 1800s had been enlarged and were displayed on the wall. One particularly charming photo was of the 1934 school band in full regalia. A large plaque covering half the wall named contributors to the successful restoration.

A secretary was hard at work in one of the well-lit offices. She informed us that the board met upstairs. "Take the elevator down the hall and when you get off, the board room will be right in front of you." We did and it was.

The room was large with chairs in rows to accommodate the large crowd and tables off to the side for additional, less involved visitors. One man was reading the paper while waiting for the board to return from executive session. We engaged him in discussion and he said he visited often, usually to the end, since his wife was on the board. This was her third year and he was certain she would want to talk to me. Although she was not one of my targeted subjects, the idea seemed appealing, if only to find out what she would say. Trustees seem eager to talk, no matter what the question!

Citizens entered by two's and three's from 7:00 P.M. to 7:30 P.M., greeting each other warmly, often giving each other hugs. There were at least forty-five visitors. Next to the sign-in sheet was a packet of information for visitors; it included the agenda of the meeting, the minutes of two prior meetings, details about the proclamations and celebrations that were to begin the meeting (which explained the reason for so many happy visitors), and information about a tornado evacuation plan for the schools. (It was one of the most complete packets for the audience I've seen.)

The room was large, with a high, patterned ceiling, freshly painted white and mauve. The board dais was raised, enabling all members of the leadership team to be highly visible. On the floor and to the left was a secretary with a portable computer; on the right was the assistant superintendent, available to answer questions. A young woman was at the far right of the board. She was poised and attentive, but never participated in the meeting. Later we learned she is a high school student who represents the student body at board meetings.

The board spent the first thirty minutes with celebrations and proclamations in honor of teachers and parents who had participated in a drug use prevention program. When they moved to more serious business, the majority of the audience left.

Rural District

The board member could be reached at his place of work, said the superintendent's secretary. In such a small community, there seemed to be no need to stand on ceremony. Reluctantly, the soft-spoken gentleman agreed to an interview, even though he hadn't been on the board long and didn't know what he could say that would be useful. When reassured that his information was valued, he agreed to an interview prior to the budget hearing and board meeting. He provided clear directions to the meeting room, including the inevitable, "You can't miss it!"

Traveling from the metropolitan area toward the Texas Hill Country through a historical and popular German community, my assistant and I felt as though we were time-traveling to a quieter, simpler era. The school building on the side of the highway was, indeed, the most conspicuous building in town. The trustee was right: we couldn't miss it!

We parked in front of a stone monolith that had names of students who had died, with their dates of birth and death; the austere monument provided a daily reminder of mortality to all who passed by.

Arriving exactly at 5:00 P.M., we walked up the concrete steps, through the second set of double-glass doors, into a simple, two-story, brick building where we were met by the young board member dressed "Texas-style" down to his "gimmie cap." The board room where we were holding the interview was on the left, opposite the superintendent's office. The superintendent greeted us, chatted for awhile, then went about his business in the office, returning later with refreshments for the board meeting.

As is common in small schools, the board room and administration building are all part of the high school. We were fascinated with the traditional school building, which included old-fashioned blackboards, varnished wooden floors, and twentieth-century technology. The board room where the interview was conducted was sparsely furnished with ten folding chairs placed around a standard conference table. There was only room for a few visitors on the couch and folding chairs, a compromise between inhospitable and welcoming.

The novice board member spoke quickly and intensely, so the interview was finished in less than forty-five minutes. Our informal conversation expanded to include other board members and the superintendent as they drifted in. The six new members on the board were all present at 6:00 P.M. for the budget hearing; the two experienced board members arrived at 6:20 P.M. and 6:30 P.M. Obviously, the budget was not controversial, because no citizens appeared for the public hearing.

Since they couldn't proceed with the regular meeting (the board meeting was posted for 7:00 P.M. and couldn't legally begin until then), the board members spent the time enjoying the light supper and chatting about families, their own children, and business affairs. It was an affable group with no signs of tension.

BEFORE YOU RUN FOR OFFICE . . .

> Wanted: Dedicated, compassionate, and hard-working men and women for a difficult and complex job that involves long hours, short tempers, and no pay. The rewards: a well-run district and a high-quality educational program for the students in our public schools!

Trustees describe their role as frustrating, fulfilling, maddening, enlightening, wonderful, aggravating, and rewarding! It's a complex, ambiguous role, requiring long hours and providing little rewards. School directors must demonstrate political skills, perform under pressure, and be able to manage conflict; "those who fear conflict will find leadership a burdensome, threatening task. Leadership brings no answer to the table. It does come with questions and a disturbing sense of unease" (Terry, 1993, p. 260).

Why do citizens want to be a member of a local school board? They tell me:

- I was "electable and knowledgeable."
- I want to make a difference for kids.

- I was talked into running for a seat.
- I contacted a school board member and expressed my displeasure and the board member said if I was not happy I ought to be part of the solution instead of complaining about the problem.
- I was recruited by a principal, board member, teacher, citizens. I care about the kids. I don't know a lot about budget, but I care about the kids. I won by twelve votes—unopposed.

Candidates may be upset about something that happened at school; they may be distressed about ever-rising taxes; they're frustrated with the current members; or they simply want to make a difference for kids. Sometimes the citizen has been encouraged to run by incumbents; often they are selected to *oppose* another candidate or incumbent.

> I didn't really know about boards. I've been on parish council, but I'm not a politician. It's OK not to like politics, but I wanted to become involved, express concerns. I like to help in whatever area I can. I have to be involved. I really didn't give it a whole lot of thought, but I'd been complaining about different things and I talked to my boss (my wife) and she said I ought to. She encouraged me to run. I've lived here all my life and know the area. I come from lower class, where there are more drop-outs. Hispanics and lower class citizens—I've been there. I managed to graduate, though, and I want to help the kids.

Trustees described the personal qualities they bring to the board with pride. They describe themselves as having a positive attitude—"Look for the good, not for the bad"—and high standards—"We want everything to be great!" "When you do something, do it right the first time." They value education and feel they can make a difference.

> Two years ago I went to a board meeting about some touchy items. There was a perception of athletes misbehaving when on the road. I testified to the board. I had a perception that the board had the power to make the decision. After two or three complaints over the telephone, I learned that I couldn't do this by myself; this needed to be a board decision.

Although controversy renews the community interest in selecting and promoting qualified and capable citizens as board candidates, trustees must make decisions over many facets of the complex business of education. The campaign should not focus on a single issue, discharging the coach, for example, since there are many other issues on the board's agenda.

> Last school year I participated as part of a community committee to hire an athletic director. One board member chaired the committee and I talked with other board members about what they did. It helped me to understand the responsibilities and duties of a board member.

Before you agree to run for trustee, consider your answers to the following questions:

- Do you believe in public schools?
- Do you understand the role of the board?
- Will you respect and guard the integrity of the governance process?
- Will you focus on important issues?
- Are you willing to set and evaluate policies, allowing the administrator and staff to implement them?
- Can you work cooperatively, working out interpersonal conflicts?
- Can you accept criticism and conflict?
- Are you honest and sincere?
- Are you open-minded?
- Are you punctual and courteous?
- Can you perform under pressure?
- Are you able to work with others to accomplish your goals?
- Are you willing to abide by the board-adopted code of ethics?
- Will you take responsibility for your own actions?
- Do you anticipate problems and act before an issue becomes urgent or critical?
- Can you tolerate ambiguity and dissonance?

Because, as a corporate body, each trustee must collaborate

with all others to achieve personal objectives, wise candidates do not impugn motives and character flaws on incumbents; it is better to focus on the positive. It is difficult enough to learn such a complex role and perform it adequately without being encumbered with campaign promises that would be illegal or inappropriate to carry out. Candidates and voters must focus on the larger issues of governance: setting goals, establishing effective policies, and allocating resources wisely.

Public forums allow the public to meet and visit with all candidates. Here are questions for citizens to consider asking aspiring trustees:

- What would you like this board to do to improve student learning?
- How can our elected officials better learn of the wishes of the community regarding our public schools?
- What policies would you like to see adopted regarding parental involvement in education?
- How would you describe the role of the school board?
- What is your position regarding the separation of church and state?
- What are your beliefs regarding assessment of student progress? Do you believe that standardized tests are an effective way to assess student progress? Do you favor alternative assessments? Why or why not?
- What involvement have you had with our public schools recently? What involvement do you plan in the future if you are not elected?
- Do you have children in our public schools? If not, why are you interested in governing the public schools?
- What ideas do you have to increase community involvement in our public schools?
- Are you familiar with our current policy regarding review of curricular materials? What would you change, if anything?

Trustees advise every board candidate to:

- Attend board meetings.

- Sit down with the superintendent (maybe principals, too) and talk about what a good quality school trustee is and does.
- "Be involved, well, maybe that's not a good word—maybe take an interest in school system, not just having kids in school, that's different."

Usually, candidates learn about the role of a school trustee from conversations with school superintendents, incumbent trustees, personal and/or professional experiences, parent activities, and/or attending state and national workshops and conventions. Hopefully, they will have attended *many* board meetings. This "anticipatory socialization" prepares the individual as he or she learns the role expectations shared and valued by the incumbents.

Many districts take advantage of the time between the dates of filing and election to prepare candidates for the role, enabling individuals to anticipate the role more accurately. General information about boardsmanship is available from many state board associations. Descriptions of the roles and responsibilities of the local school board from the local policy manual or current booklets from the state school board's association may be provided to all candidates. Recent board packets, a copy of the board-adopted code of ethics, community demographics, student handbooks, and recent test data is essential. An introduction to the staff and a tour of facilities provides context for the role.

We must share the true job description of the local school board and the challenges of governance. All candidates should have at least an overview of the roles and responsibilities of the local board within state guidelines, possibly available through local board policy. Half-hearted candidates may decide not to campaign when they have a better understanding of the vast amount of knowledge and high level of skills required for effective performance.

All candidates should be clear about how the board operates, consider the purpose of the board to be personally important, and understand the board's mission. Even for unsuccessful candidates, making this information readily available benefits everyone. *All* citizens should understand the relationship between effective school governance and quality education. The campaign can focus on governance issues, not personalities, when all interested parties understand the importance of this policy-making body in providing success for all students.

QUALITY CANDIDATES

Persons once brought status to the board; today they become a member of the board to *achieve* status.

Schlechty, 1990

Although members of school boards are thought to be representative of their communities, the composite portrait of the school trustee has not changed with the changing demographics throughout the country. A typical trustee is likely to be a white, male, suburban homeowner whose age and annual income fall in the forties. He has a professional job, advanced degrees, and children who attend public schools. He is more likely to represent the civic leadership, not the community as a whole, especially when elected at-large (Freeman, 1991).

Trustees with a background in education or on another governing board may fit very comfortably with the incumbents, but newcomers with diverse skills, background, and experiences enable the board to move beyond the status quo.

Where do we find such willing and able citizens?

Just as "it takes a whole village to raise a child," so must the community work together to *create the conditions* that attract a large pool of candidates who have the qualities and capacity for effective performance in the role. Civic leaders, including incumbent trustees, should encourage able parents and other potential candidates to serve on district or campus committees to become knowledgeable about the district. Experience as a member on similar boards or participation in other aspects of public education (PTA, volunteer activities, campus improvement teams) provides a solid background and enables voters to observe talent in action. Business leaders who support school improvement must encourage their employees to serve on local boards by providing support and release time for campaign and board service.

The necessity for integrity and wisdom, critical thinking, and conflict management skills is evident considering the need for an informed and skillful political body to guide our educational system toward excellence. When *all* our candidates have *capacity* for educational leadership, *represent all segments* of the community, and *accept the challenges* of this complex and ambiguous role, the board will continually improve.

CHAPTER 3

Overcoming the Personal Challenges

ADVICE FOR THE NOVICE TRUSTEE

The hardest thing is the way you are treated. Before the election I was just a parent, now that I am a school board member, teachers are more aware. I want to be treated as a whole person, not just a board member. I am not watching every move that teachers are making and I want teachers to know that is not part of my job. I am watching out for the district, not trying to find the bad in every teacher or staff member.

YOU must first manage these personal changes before you will be able to deal with the social ones, such as pressures from constituents. Most newly-elected trustees are treated differently by the community and the educational staff after the election. Your ability to handle your new pressures and prestige will determine to a large extent how happy you will be while serving as a member of a board. You must manage the loss of your former identity as engineer, parent, or salesperson and keep the new role of school trustee from becoming your whole identity.

In the grocery store, the office, and the neighborhood, listen courteously to congratulations, curious comments, and (perhaps) directives and make no commitments. Instead, respond with neutral comments. Telephone calls, angry or inquisitive neighbors, and frustrated educators may inundate you with requests and complaints. You must continually remind others (and possibly, yourself) that you are only *one* member of a corporate body. *You have no individual authority!* Unless the board has requested that you represent them in some way, you have power only when the board is in session.

Consider these sample responses to queries, demands, and complaints:

- I look forward to becoming more knowledgeable about our schools.
- I'm certain it will be a challenge, but I'll do my best.
- Thank you for sharing your concern. Be certain to talk to (name the appropriate person in the chain of command) about it.

Then, as you always have, inquire about the *other* person's health and well-being (or their children's!). If you remind them of your other (mutual) interests and activities, they will be more likely to allow you to remain a complete and multi-faceted human being.

Even though you will want to be responsive to your constituents, do not allow the telephone to become a tyrant in your household, or you may never again eat a hot meal! Investing in an answering machine will pay off in peace of mind.

When you return the calls, listen courteously and, as soon as you can, find out why the person is calling, so you can make a decision about how to handle the caller. Information calls are easy, but complainers must be reminded of the chain of command and the board's policy regarding grievances. You may need to inform the caller of the fact that you cannot take sides without jeopardizing your ability to serve as an impartial hearing officer if the board eventually is to render a judgment.

If the caller has a serious concern regarding questionable behavior or an emergency, of course notify the superintendent and board president as soon as possible! Ask experienced trustees how to discourage a steady stream of callers, since most of the concerns should be directed to, and handled by, members of the educational staff.

PRESSURES ON THE FAMILY

Assuming this very public role may exact a toll on family relationships as well as your personal and professional life. Because the board is the largest employer and financial supporter of local businesses in many communities, board decisions become highly personal. It is difficult to be in fellowship with the family of a non-renewed teacher or maintain a golf foursome with a friend whose business did not receive an important contract.

On the other hand, family members become an informal communication link to school events for trustees. "My wife is a school teacher. The only thing that I was not aware of was what happened in executive session." One trustee felt her "children are treated better. Teachers know the parents care about the child enough to know they are going to do everything possible to make learning a better experience."

One mother said the decision to run for the board position was made "as a family, because there will be a definite effect on the children. You cannot go up to school to scream and holler. Kids have to be *good.*"

It can be a handicap to family members in other ways. One trustee's sister lost an employment opportunity because he was a member of the local board.

A popular board trainer, now Superintendent of Lago Vista ISD, Texas, Dr. Jess Butler, uses this story to illustrate the impact of board decisions on family relationships:

The board was involved in acrimonious debate over "closed" or "open" campuses.

Everyone had an opinion: his wife's brother ran the nearby fast-food emporium, his daughter had just received her driver's license, and his boss owned the bowling alley nearby that catered to the loitering, flirting students during lunch.

However, students had been injured while off campus for lunch and teachers complained that students were returning late from lunch, often high or drunk. In spite of pressure from family and friends, Mr.

Jones voted with the narrow majority to close the high school campus during lunch.

One friend and admirer said. "Wow! What courage! There's a man who can sleep at night!"

"Yes," said another, "but where?"

Work with family members to deal with the many demands on your time; they can be your strongest supporters. Alert them to the possibility that they may be spotlighted and targeted, and discuss how to manage phone calls and angry or inquisitive friends and neighbors. Even your children must learn how to manage inappropriate comments and how to take phone calls courteously without getting involved in discussions.

Wise trustees garner support and encouragement from all family members and have regular discussions about managing inappropriate remarks, pressures, and expectations from citizens. Keeping your public role separate from your family life may save them some grief when, sooner or later, you will make an unpopular decision. Refraining from discussing board business at home enables all members of the family to respond truthfully, "I wouldn't know anything about that. My dad/mom never discusses that stuff at home."

TIME REQUIREMENTS

Managing time and information is a problem for all new trustees. Even those who attended board meetings prior to election find the amount of information and time requirements overwhelming. Time formerly devoted to social and family life may be seriously curtailed by new responsibilities:

> They told me two meetings a month and some reading. "I can do that. No problem." When I got in, I found out there's a lot more to it!

Some boards meet monthly for a few hours. Others, usually urban boards, meet every other week. But, regular board meetings of three to eight hours may be only the tip of the iceberg. Special meetings, committee meetings, emergency meetings, executive sessions, orientation sessions, and union negotiations will make great demands on your time. Special circumstances, such as hiring a new superintendent, campus construction, and discipline or budget hearings demand even more meetings.

There are numerous social functions relating to the role. Trustees may be expected to make presentations as part of a public relations team or represent the board during a bond issue campaign. Board development programs require evenings and weekends, but few complain about ceremonial occasions such as graduations and award banquets!

INFORMATION MANAGEMENT

> Preparing and getting ready for every meeting that we have, there's just so much to read, so much you need to be knowledgeable on, that I had no idea when I decided to run that there was so much involved.

Education is, by definition, an information-intensive industry. Even when you are home, you may be reading—the board packet, proposals, recommendations, and publications. Keeping up with vast quantities of information will accelerate your effectiveness. In addition to district memos and newsletters, you will receive information from state and national associations. You could quickly become overwhelmed with all this information. Learn to scan for important information and read for details only on crucial issues.

> I need more study time. They throw so much at you and you don't have the skills to discriminate between important and unimportant information. I'd like to have a sense of what was important, if the information could be summarized, even prioritized, I'd know what mattered. The other day I spent two to three hours reading about something only to be told, well, that's not important. Well, there goes two to three hours of my time.

Some superintendents flood the board with information, causing the trustees to become overwhelmed. This allows the superintendent to challenge them in board meetings and discourage any probing questions! "Didn't you read that in the information I've provided you?" (Heller and Rancic, October, 1993). Such behavior is not only counterproductive but unethical and needs to be addressed by the board as a whole.

Instead of inundating boards with detail and reams of statistics, wise superintendents provide executive summaries and sources for additional information for those who wish it. Striking a balance between providing too much and not enough information should be discussed by the board and superintendent. Those trustees who have minimal reading skills might need a verbal overview of the board packet.

Although some individuals require more data than others, the board as a whole should agree on appropriate kinds and amounts of information necessary for good governance. Individual trustees sometimes use requests for information to manipulate the superintendent and staff. When one trustee asks for information the rest of the board does not need, it implies micromanagement, not governance. The larger issue probably is trust: "We don't believe the superintendent's report, so we'll get *all* the information from the *last five years!*" Individuals may need to be reminded of the importance of acting together as a board.

If, after reading over the board packet, you need more information, ask for it well ahead of time. It is your responsibility to be certain that you have enough information to make wise governance decisions. If the district is only beginning to discuss alternative school calendars, for example, trustees need only introductory information. If the board plans to vote on a year-round calendar for their district at this meeting, however, they may need more information.

Learn to manage the deluge of paper by following these three steps:

- Do it!
- File it! or
- Throw it away!

Experienced trustees say it becomes easier to move quickly to step three as the quantity of information grows. They advise you not to keep any document if someone else has a copy; otherwise you will need to buy not only more filing cabinets but add storage space to your living quarters! Deciding *what* to save will be easier over time.

LEARNING AS YOU GO

J. P., a typical trustee, said his first orientation was at convention six weeks after his election. Other information about his role came weekly from the superintendent's office. Notes and thoughts for trustees include state and local information, news clippings, the TASB Bulletin, the Texas Superintendent Insider, and information about the district's schools such as calendars and memoranda from the principals.

New members are expected to jump right in and carry the board's agenda forward while learning educational jargon, board procedures, and "the way we do things around here." The greater the difference between the novice's managerial and organizational experience and the management and nature of the district, the more orientation is needed. Without a pre-service or orientation program, it is estimated that it will take six to twelve months of on-the-job experience before the trustee can perform effectively.

Race, age, gender, and educational status influence early performance. For example, professionals may expect deferential treatment from those with fewer credentials, and less educated trustees often defer to the greater expertise of the superintendent, discounting their own experiences and failing to contribute in essential ways. Those who have experience in education, visit board meetings prior to election, work with educators on committees, or have experiences on other boards are more confident about their ability to perform well and manage the inherent pressures (Rosenberger, 1993).

However, no matter how much pre-socialization has taken place, there is much to learn before being thrust into "active, often turbulent environments" (Institute of Educational Leadership, 1986). Everyone experiences the phenomenon known as "job shock" as a result of the discrepancy between the perceived and actual role and responsibilities.

- I had no idea that . . .
- It makes no sense that . . .
- I've tried to understand, but . . .
- When you are an observer, you don't understand the rules of the state. You just ask, "Well, why can't you do this? Why can't you do that?" And you never know why. Although there are some people that say, "Well, just do it anyway." It is difficult to understand.
- Got in, found out there's a lot more to it. Knowledgeable superintendent, secretary is very helpful, answers questions, personnel director, virtually everybody there has been helpful, staff, anything I need.
- Almost everything is new to me—relationship of administrator and board was confusing. I was under the impression the board ruled, but the board really is the policymaker.

Most believe that the board had more say in running the schools. They are surprised to learn how the board role is severely constrained by state laws, judicial decisions, legislative actions, and limited resources. In addition, they are unaware of the extent of information and skills they must have to make informed decisions regarding district operations. Unfortunately (and sometimes contrary to legal mandates), half received no training prior to their first meeting.

> The night that I was elected to the board, I was given a piece of advice by a member who was serving her third term. She told me, for the first year, to keep my mouth shut and my ears open. This was probably the best piece of advice that I have ever totally ignored. With no formal training or even a slight clue about what I was doing, I hit the ground running. Like so many others who have jumped into the fray, I had never attended a school board meeting and had little idea what the issues were.

> The Idaho State School Board Association attempted to help with a film strip made in the sixties. I learned by many hours of reading and countless telephone calls to teachers, administrators, and the boards.

Many newcomers share this sense of being overwhelmed; experienced trustees say they weren't qualified to govern well until the third year. These policymakers must learn an incredible amount of information rapidly. In addition to the technical aspects (the "what" of the board's work), the novice must simultaneously learn the "how" — the norms and standard operating procedures of the current board. This may be the most difficult task of the newcomer, since the operating values are powerful but invisible and unspoken. "The way we do things 'round here" defines the board's behavior, activities, and rules. These shared social expectations are norms to be respected and complied with, and incumbents may get upset when things are done differently.

Because few have the benefit of a comprehensive orientation, trustees learn their role through a combination of informal and formal learning opportunities, a notoriously ineffective and inefficient method.

> I always learn a lot just from talking to people. I have a mind of my own. But I listen to others and think, "That's right!"

> I spoke with several people who said in the first year you'll be very nervous; sit back, kind of listen and take everything in; find out where you stand and where you need to go.

Success in this important role should not be left up to the motivation and attitude of each newcomer. Making wise decisions about highly complex, emotional, and political topics in a public setting requires a high level of interpersonal skills and a vast amount of information not known to most lay leaders. Often novices will see themselves as the source or cause of events when external factors are responsible. From current or former trustees they learn that confusion and misunderstandings are common to everyone, enabling them to feel more comfortable and less anxious.

EFFECTIVE ORIENTATION

Some states *require* board orientation, but even without a mandate, wise superintendents and board presidents provide for orientation *every time* there is a new member. Unfortunately, because of time demands, lack of motivation, or a need to maintain control, many superintendents neglect this important task even when they are legally required to do so.

> I don't want this to reflect on our administration or anything, but I wish I had more on-site, hands-on training. I haven't pursued it and I know he would tell me, but, well, more hand-holding in the earlier stages would have helped. I'm having to get this on my own and I don't want to ask them too much, I'm afraid I may bother them. But if they were proactive it would have been better.
>
> MR[1]: It sounds like you're saying, "if I knew what the questions were, I'd have asked them."
>
> That's right. I've been to six to eight board meetings and I feel like a dummy when some things come up. The first year, I guess you're just supposed to nod at times and vote the best you can.

An effective orientation program assists newcomers by providing opportunities to acquire both content knowledge and process skills. They must quickly learn their role and how to work together within legal and policy guidelines to accomplish their objectives. Above all, the trustee needs a copy of (or access to) the policy manual and information about its origin and importance!

Many superintendents discount a need for formal orientation by saying, "I maintain an open-door policy. If the trustee has a question they can just stop by." Such an attitude is flawed since it leaves the burden of training on the novice, assuming not only that the newcomer knows what to ask but is able to discriminate among myriad details. If the trustee doesn't have a comfortable relationship with the superintendent he/she may be even more reluctant to ask many questions.

James Lehman, formerly Superintendent of Weslaco ISD, Texas, provides an outstanding orientation, using a handbook with a table of contents similar to this one:

Overview of Boardsmanship
  • Your Powers and Duties as a School Trustee

---

[1]MR refers to the author.

- Board's Responsibilities
- Board Training Requirements

Overview of the District
- Site-Based Management
- The Business Office
  Budget
  Accounts Payable
  Tax Collection/Assessment
  Salaries
  Benefits
  State Support
  Paying Teachers
- The Personnel Office
  Personnel and Pupil Services Staff
  District Staffing Allocations
  Staffing Professional Employees
  Teacher Induction
  Staffing Paraprofessional Employees
  Staffing Hourly Support Employees
  Pay Proposals
  Payroll Computations
  Teacher Appraisals
  Career Ladder
  Contract Renewals for Professional Employees
  Contract Non-Renewals for Professional Employees
  Dismissal of Professional Employees
  Affirmative Action
- Maintenance/Operation
  Tour of all School Facilities
  Shopping List of Needs: Roofs and Major Facilities

The Curriculum and Instruction Office
  Instructional Oversight and Coordination
  Curriculum
  Gifted and Talented
  Special Education
  Bilingual—ESL
  Compensatory Education

Even Start
Applied Technology Education
Student Assistance Programs
Summer School
Accreditation and Compliance
State Board of Education – Southern Association of
  Standards
State Board of Education Rules for Curriculum
District Instructional Goals
Campus Improvement Plans
Textbook Adoption
Board Policy Coordination
Discipline Management
State Compensatory Program

Other details every policymaker should know include:

- the standard procedures of the local board including meeting process, how the board meeting agenda is created, public participation, and use of the consent agenda
- superintendent contract, job description, the results of the most recent board evaluation, and current goals
- current data on educational programs and district demographics
- legal issues facing the board
- other sources of information for trustees, such as the State School Board Association, National School Board Association (NSBA), educational journals and publications, and the state education agency

The superintendent and board president should create a listing such as this one and update and adapt it as necessary. Such a list also may serve as a needs assessment, allowing the novice to build on his/her prior knowledge and related experiences. For example, a maintenance engineer might want to spend more time learning about current personnel issues; insurance agents might spend more time on operations and maintenance; current and former educators may need fewer sessions regarding programs and more on financial concerns. Using staff members to assist in this induction process enables the trustee to develop relationships as well as expertise.

Although the board can't cease its business during this ongoing orientation process, the board will be able to continue its ongoing duties with a minimum of disruption when it demonstrates respect and support for the novice. Because the newcomer cannot learn everything all at once, ongoing support, advice, and suggestions should be available from a current or former trustee. Incumbents provide the newcomer with relevant and reliable information to interpret events. Often it is the newer members who are most helpful, since trustees with five or more years of experience have lost track of the amount of information they have learned over the years. However, if trustees sit in the same position regularly, newcomers should be seated near a strong policymaker, not a weak one, since many trustees learn much about their role in casual conversations with incumbents, before, during and after meetings.

Skillful superintendents socialize new members to maintain established norms and prevent having the novice learn undesirable beliefs and behaviors. Trustees are more likely to ask questions of the superintendent if they have a positive relationship with him/her. If highly motivated and committed, the newcomer will supplement the official orientation with books, journal articles, and the policy manual.

As a result of the orientation process, every trustee should have the answers to the following questions:

- What must I know before my first board meeting?
- To whom do I go with concerns and suggestions for improvements?
- Who creates the agenda for each board meeting? How would I go about placing an item on the agenda?
- How can I ensure good working relationships with other trustees? The superintendent? Staff?
- Are there standing board committees? If so, what are their responsibilities, charges, and memberships?
- What board-adopted policies will assist me in responding

to complaints from citizens? What should I do when citizens or staff members bring complaints?

- Which policies are key to my effectiveness as a member of this board?
- How does the board know whether its policies are implemented?
- Does the district have a strategic plan? When was it created? Based on that plan, what are the district's major goals and objectives?
- What changes has this district undergone in the last year? Five years? What changes are anticipated? What plans are being made to manage these changes?
- How does the board influence the school curriculum?
- *When* are school programs evaluated? *How* are they evaluated?
- What are the district's ground rules for determining what is board business and what is staff work?
- How does this board plan for its own evaluation and improvement?
- What do I need to know about relationships with unions? Pending contracts and negotiations?

A trustee doesn't need all the details of the educational program, but when newcomers have been informed of recent executive sessions, legal and personal *faux pas* may be avoided. It is the responsibility of the superintendent and board president to select critical issues and bring the novice up to speed as soon as possible. The novice who ran on a platform of "no new taxes" will undoubtedly be surprised by the many unfunded state mandates. Even those who have attended board meetings regularly may not know the relevance of the district's strategic plan and budget cycle on this week's agenda.

Unfortunately, because of the timing of trustee elections, some newcomers join the board during the final stages of the budget process. If the novice has not attended public hearings prior to being sworn in as trustee, he/she may not be able to participate knowledgeably in the final vote. Making wise decisions regarding allocation of resources during times of shrinking budgets requires knowledge of budgets, tax rates, bond issues, and complex decision-making skills.

Usually a newcomer doesn't know what the rules are until he/she breaks one – an unfortunate, often embarrassing, learning experience. Sunshine laws, the legal aspects of meeting management, and past agendas must be explained to avoid missteps and possible legal issues.

One superintendent learned the necessity of filling in background information for novice trustees during "the moment of truth" at a board workshop. The superintendent had been severely constrained by the board and didn't know why. Finally, one of the newcomers asked why he had transferred principals from one campus to another. This gave the superintendent the opportunity to tell the trustee that he had been directed to exchange principals by the prior board *in executive session.* The superintendent didn't know the problem and the trustees didn't know the background information. When the explanation for the mix-up was understood, the animosity fell away and harmony was restored.

ADVOCATING FOR IMPROVED PROGRAMS

> An invasion of armies can be resisted,
> but not an idea whose time has come.
>
> Victor Hugo

Because no individual member can determine policy or commit the board to action, each trustee must develop coalitions with other trustees to accomplish worthwhile goals. Each must find common interests and negotiate differences.

You have a brilliant idea. Say, as a professional in the technology field, you know that the district's technology is way behind the market. You want the district to modernize its career education program. How do you, as an individual trustee, make it happen? (You do not, of course, bring it up as a surprise at the next board meeting or write a nasty letter to the local newspaper.)

Perhaps, as a parent, you have reviewed the district's course descriptions and graduation requirements and visited with the director of the career education department. As a novice (and eager!) trustee, you have reviewed the materials you were provided at orientation and discovered that upgrading the technology program is one of the five-year goals.

You schedule a visit with the superintendent and the board president to share your interest and concern. You are clear about your expected outcome, long- and short-range. As the proponent of the issue, you are prepared to justify, explain, and support your passion. You share models of success, such as other districts' programs, as well as resources and opportunities to overcome barriers.

Your meeting with the superintendent results in one of the following scenarios:

- The board president and superintendent convince you that the cost is prohibitive and you agree to table the issue (for the time being).
- Both the board president and superintendent feel it is a low priority item and discourage your taking further action. At your insistence, it is placed on the board agenda but the other trustees refuse to discuss the issue, disparage your involvement, and your motion for a task force dies for lack of a second.
- The board president and superintendent share your concern and place it as a discussion item on the next board agenda. From visiting, informally, with other trustees, you learn that some share your concerns, while others are neutral or negative about the issue. You offer to provide materials and information for the board supporting the need for current technology for all children. After a brief discussion at the board meeting, the board approves a request for the superintendent to create a task force to review the issue and bring recommendations to the board within three months.

The first scenario is the most discouraging, leaving you to consider other options. As a policymaker, your role is to ensure the board-adopted goals are implemented, not to carry them out yourself. Because building a technology program was adopted as a district goal, it is appropriate for you to discuss their resistance at your next board workshop. If that goal has already been delegated to the superintendent it becomes an item to discuss during the superintendent's evaluation, as well.

Another item that should be discussed at the next board evaluation and training session is the lack of support from the other trustees during the meeting. Was there information you should have had prior to the board meeting? Did other trustees feel you were out-of-order in bringing forth the issue? Perhaps your timing was off and the board wanted it discussed at a later time — perhaps during budget hearings.

INTELLECTUAL INTEGRITY

Effective trustees work under public scrutiny and are gracious under stress. However, in my work, I find novice trustees resisting the axiom from James McGregor Burns (1978) that leaders must be willing to make unpopular decisions. Terry (1993) adds, "Those who fear conflict will find leadership a burdensome, threatening task, for true leadership requires authenticity and integrity: a congruence of beliefs and behavior" (p. 282). Each newcomer must fit his/her personal belief system within the imbedded expectations of the role. "The ego diminishes, allowing for the servant-leader and the stewardship of the common good" (Terry, 1993, p. 282).

Because "silence means consent," the individual must participate within the group, insisting that others clarify their ideas, interrupting the stream of talk to insert one's own question or to raise a counterpoint. As Smith and Berg (1987) remind us, "It requires courage to find one's own voice in a group, to speak with personal authority in the presence of institutional authority" (p. 147).

It also requires doing the work necessary to contribute to the discussion and willingness to trust one's own judgment. When an individual is overwhelmed or intimidated by the power of the group, the group will lack that person's insight and function at a lower intellectual level.

> If I didn't understand something, I worked at it until I did, because there was no point in taking on any task unless I could contribute to it. It was sometimes embarrassing to have to stop the discussion and say, "Wait a minute . . . I don't understand that. What am I missing?" But most people respect an honest question and love expanding on their particular area of expertise.
>
> Conway (1994), p. 221

Integrity and wisdom, critical thinking, and decision-making skills are essential skills for trustees. Because few decisions are easy, ethical decision making is based on doing your homework and getting the facts. Review relevant documents and speak to knowledgeable folk who will help you in separating fact from fiction. You might have to consult policy manuals, minutes of past meetings, and other documents. If you need to interpret some legalese, consult your board attorney.

List several potential actions you could take and assess the consequences of each proposal. Look at precedents and review past experiences in order to increase the accuracy of your projected results. (Of course you will easily eliminate those that are clearly illegal or unrealistic.) What short- and long-term effects will each possible action have? Is your decision consistent with past practices and policies or will this be precedent-setting? After you have thoughtfully considered the facts, possible consequences, and effects on others, make the decision you can ethically defend.

"Leadership," says Terry (1993), "does not expect roses; it lives with thorns. Yet is hope filled" (p. 272). Effective boardsmanship requires a true blend of team leadership, authentic communication, and courage.

BOARD SELF-EVALUATION

(*1*) Does the leadership team provide a comprehensive orientation for all notice trustees?   Yes_____ No_____

(2) Does every notice trustee have an assigned mentor?
                                                        Yes_____ No_____

CHAPTER 4

Learning a Complex, Ill-Defined Role

> Two things seemed pretty apparent: one was that in order to be a Mississippi River pilot a man has got to learn more than any one man ought to be allowed to know and the other was, that he must learn it all over again in a different way every 24 hours.
>
> Mark Twain

LIKE Mark Twain on the river, trustees face the challenge of continuously learning a poorly defined and ever-changing role. At their first board meeting, unaware of the complexities of school finance, district policies, contract administration, and school law, novice trustees are expected to make informed decisions about controversial subjects.

Although we recognize the complex tasks school boards are to do—establish policy, allocate resources, select a superintendent, and so on—there is precious little in our board development programs to assist public citizens in becoming experts in educational governance. These lay leaders are not expected to possess the professional knowledge of educators, but they must learn an incredible amount of information rapidly.

Making wise decisions about highly complex, emotional, and political topics in a public setting requires a high level of interpersonal skills and a vast amount of information. The public expects trustees to make wise decisions in ambiguous situations under tight time constraints! Yet few trustees receive the quality of training provided for business and industry leaders—across the country, board training is notoriously fragmented, episodic, and shallow (Carver, 1991; Gibboney, 1991; IEL, 1986).

This training void leaves trustees to learn their role through a combination of informal and formal learning opportunities. The results are then determined by the interest, motivation, and attitude of each trustee. Most commonly she will learn on the job through trial and error (notoriously ineffective and inefficient). If highly motivated and committed, she may supplement whatever orientation she has received with books, journal articles, and the policy manual. She may ask questions of the superintendent if she has a positive relationship with him/her. She may select a mentor, usually a current or former trustee, even though the mentor may have obsolete information. Conferences and literature from the state and national school board associations provide information about the wider world of education.

The risk of this do-it-yourself method is exacerbated by the common condition of not knowing what we don't know or "secondary ignorance." Often the history and or context of the discussion has been assimilated into the shared information of the incumbents, who are not aware that they are using a form of verbal shorthand, including acronyms and buzz words that have no meaning to the novice. "Chapter 1," "mainstreamed," A. D. A., "504," E.S.L., and "A. R. D." aren't common terms outside of the educational field, and until new trustees understand such terms, they can't even formulate an intelligent sounding question. In order to be perceived as competent, they pretend to know what's being discussed, behaving as if they are knowledgeable and informed.

Pretending to know everything at public school board meetings has a predictable negative effect on the quality of decision making, problem solving, and communication. The basic human need to overcome feelings of inadequacy encourages trustees to grab hold of issues where they can display some expertise and avoid discussion they don't understand. As they fall into the habit of dealing with organizational, financial, and procedural matters, they neglect their primary function of governing the schools.

It is time we stopped teaching trustees how to maintain the status quo. We must provide them with executive level leadership training programs to support them in becoming an effective governing body. Then they will stop dealing with "bursted boilers" and get into educational matters. Without such skill development, school boards are relegated to remaining "incompetent groups of competent people."

CREATING A COMPREHENSIVE BOARD DEVELOPMENT PROGRAM

A comprehensive board development program is based on these assumptions:

- Boardsmanship is a highly complex, continually evolving responsibility and trustees should receive assistance in mastering the role.
- All school trustees wish to be competent and effective in school governance.
- Boards govern well when they can make sense of their situation and receive support in developing collegial relationships.
- High-performing school boards demonstrate knowledge, skills, and attitudes that can be learned by *all* school boards.
- All training sessions should develop knowledge and skills essential to effective school governance.
- Content and skills should be taught and learned at increasing levels of expertise.
- The board should continually monitor their performance and select the training opportunities that will meet their assessed needs.

Because there is no competent community if *all* members are not competent, individual trustees, as well as whole boards, must develop their abilities. The board then provides opportunities for them to share their newly acquired knowledge and skills. Although interpersonal skills may be improved individually, consensus regarding roles, relationships, and responsibilities must be worked out in board workships. Legal information, economic and national educational trends, etc., can be learned through print, media, or workshops, but the corporate body must integrate the information into its collective body of knowledge to make wise decisions for the district.

Learning the essential knowledge and skills for effective performance is a continuous process, based on regular self-evaluation by the leadership team. Boards can build their training on the results of that evaluation, using practices and skills demonstrated by high-performing boards as a standard.

A comprehensive board development program should reflect what we know from research about adults as learners. Such training requires an environment conducive to learning, an effective and knowledgeable facilitator, clearly stated learning objectives, research-based content, and time for skill practice. They must have time to reflect, to process information, not just be passive listeners!

> As an example, we had a retreat. The board had hoped we could get to know one another, set out board priorities. But the entire time was set out by the superintendent and TASB to hear lectures about the superintendent's agenda. There was absolutely zero time for any interaction.

Boards continually form and re-form as experienced members are replaced by novice trustees. So there must be skill development for individuals, as well as the entire board. For example, experienced trustees have mastered the personal concerns of the novice, described in Chapter 3, and are more interested in budget, educational programs, and ethical leadership.

A comprehensive board development program would include, but not be limited to, the following topics:

(*1*) Overview for board candidates
(*2*) Orientation for new and continuing trustees
(*3*) Efficient and productive board meetings
  • creating the agenda
  • consent agenda
  • the board-adopted rules of order

- role, responsibilities, and relationships of the board and the superintendent
- becoming a high-performing leadership team

(*4*) Governing under tight constraints
- state and local mandates
- judicial decisions
- dwindling budgets

(*5*) Governing tools
- the budget as a planning document
- evaluating the superintendent, board, staff
- the power of policies
- creating the district's vision

(*6*) The total financial picture
- the local budget process
- setting the tax rate
- state requirements and limitations

(*7*) Interpersonal skills
- communicating with each other, staff, the press, and the community
- building coalitions to accomplish objectives
- conflict management, group dynamics, and leadership skills

(*8*) The current and future educational program

(*9*) Advocacy skills

(*10*) Evaluation and accountability strategies

The content of the board training must be continually monitored, evaluated, and updated, since changing legislation and current research require new skills and information. Some state associations and curriculum developers have found advisory committees to be helpful in creating a listing of knowledge, skills, and attitudes of an effective trustee. This becomes the foundation of a comprehensive board development curriculum, beginning with an eight-hour orientation. The interactive training should combine content knowledge with the interpersonal skills essential for leadership skill development.

STATE AND NATIONAL CONFERENCES

Trustees say they learn a lot at state and national school board association conferences. These conferences use two methods of sharing information: a lecture or two (usually motivational speakers), and small break-out sessions. Because a large amount of information can be presented in a short time to a large group, lectures are cost-effective but provide no opportunity for the reflection and skill development that changes behavior.

The content of the break-out sessions at these conferences is, usually, general knowledge and showcases of innovative educational programs. Such workshops are sometimes called "drive-by training," because of their random, detached content. Most break-out topics fall in these general categories:

- labor relations
- current legislative issues
- school finance
- roles and responsibilities of boards and superintendents
- meeting management
- recruiting, hiring, and evaluating the superintendent
- school facilities
- public relations
- effective board-superintendent relations
- successful bond elections
- the hot topic du jour: gangs, dropouts, authentic assessment, etc.

A series of one-hour presentations on "Effective Meetings," "Evaluating the Superintendent," or "Roles and Responsibilities of Board Members" fails to provide the information and/or skills required for innovative leaders of educational reform and resourceful policymakers. Programs that provide only a cursory overview of the content and processes essential for informed decision making do more harm than good.

The topics and selection of speakers and presentations for such conferences could and should be as powerful and innovative as those for corporate leadership. Speakers from business, industry, higher education, and futurists, would provide the context for educational motivation.

In addition to the board-specific conferences, trustees may attend the many conferences provided by educational associations at the state and national level. Trustees attend these conferences to learn about educational programs so they can support them with policies and resources. For example, to become quickly immersed in the world of school counselors, trustees might attend their state or national conference, if only for one day. By listening to the major speakers and attending a few sessions, they have a sense of the nature of the work and important issues in the field (at least as the association perceives them).

These questions might be helpful to reflect on when attending any conference:

- How much information is based on well-done research and how much is opinion and/or rhetoric?
- Is this conference primarily concerned with students' needs?
- Is the focus on the past or the future?
- What are the perceived challenges to the profession?
- What are the "hot topics"?
- What is being done by this association at the state and national level to support student success? What is not being done?
- How do these activities compare to what is being done locally?

In addition to the formal presentations and the break-out sessions, trustees learn a lot in the halls and snack areas as they visit with other participants, learning how boards support (or hinder) programs through policies and resources.

However, learning about other districts' successful programs may open a Pandora's Box of possibilities for the eager trustee if there is no connection to district needs. Without a clear sense of his/her role, a trustee might be carried away by conference presenters who focus on implementation, not policy and resource issues. Attending conferences should be only one part of the learning process, well integrated into a total comprehensive board development program. The board then provides opportunity for the participant to discuss innovative programs and allow all to determine their applicability to the district.

CLUSTER TRAINING

Sometimes many boards come together for media presentations or lectures. Such cluster training is an efficient way to share information regarding educational, financial, or legislative issues. Facilitators who build in opportunity for reflection and dialogue multiply the effectiveness of the program. I have found that trustees respond best to workshops that provide them an opportunity for reflection and dialogue, are well-organized, and contain no "fluff." They don't appreciate an endless list of "don'ts" or being preached to. They enjoy guided discussions about the larger political, economic and social environment—the more practical and concrete the better. Workshops must be tightly organized to use the limited time well.

Trustees must make provision for the transfer of skills or knowledge to the board room. After board discussion they can decide how to use the new information to improve their performance, district plans, or educational programs. Incidental learning occurs before and after such workshops when trustees take time to compare and contrast *their* board's procedures, practices, and challenges with other boards'.

INDIVIDUAL BOARD WORKSHOPS

Although workshops and conferences are a popular method of learning a lot of information quickly, behavior change requires coaching, practice, modeling, and feedback, usually available only at *individual board workshops*. Because of sunshine laws, boards have few opportunities to know each other informally except at these workshops. Individual board workshops can create conditions for the trust and mutual respect essential for effective team leadership. Without devoting the necessary time and energy required to learn team skills, boards are unlikely to develop coalitions, identify mutually shared values, and determine common goals.

> And one of the difficulties is that the board has thus far been unable to get together in any kind of a session when the superintendent was not there so we can thrash out things between us so we can come together as a board, if we're going to come together as a board. And so, we're already in a process of defining strategies to do that.
>
> Well, what we do is talk together among ourselves. Not making decisions . . . just visiting, we have to be very careful so we're not violating the open meetings law.
>
> MR: What do you wish would have happened?
>
> That we could sit down, talk about the district, what we perceived it to be, what we perceived its problems to be, goal setting, getting a sense of where various board members might be in the sense of setting those priorities.

Such workshops are usually made available at the urging of the superintendent on a specific topic. They may be facilitated by someone from the state school board association, a professor, or an independent consultant. "Roles and Responsibilities," "Conflict Resolution," and "Board Goal-Setting" are popular. (Sample agendas are included.) The major emphasis is practical strategies to display characteristics related to effective performance or *competencies.*

Every successful workshop I have facilitated has been custom-designed by all the members of the educational leadership team. Because the trustee's motivation to learn will increase when there is a close match between the learner, the content, and the delivery system, careful preparation of the workshop supports the likelihood of success. The workship will be more successful in a safe and pleasant environment, free of interruptions. (I have always regretted a training on-site, especially during weekdays!)

THE FACILITATOR

A skilled facilitator is key. He/she must be knowledgeable in both the *content* and the *process* of governance and the social dynamics of groups. The participants must value the expertise of the facilitator. If they doubt the trainer's intentions or cannot find opportunity to express their interests and concerns, they will fail to become involved in the learning process. Trustees value "war stories" from veterans that provide the context for new skill development. As the facilitator provides background knowledge, participants are invited to ask relevant questions and reflect on the implications of this new information.

Because of diverse learning styles, the facilitator will use a variety of strategies, such as role playing, lecturettes (*short lectures, less than three minutes*), case studies, videos, and small group interactions. Isolated facts and other details can be provided as written material for later reference since the focus of training is *skill development*. The facilitator will provide opportunities that encourage speculation and creativity, as well as integrate diverse ideas. He/she may need to *frame and reframe* the issues. He/she must be skillful in unblocking overheated discussions or energizing unproductive ones. To enable the group to remember and integrate their ideas, sometimes he/she must reflect and mirror issues back to the group.

The best workshops are organized so that all trustees are able to discover their common understandings and values in order to propose new ideas and courses of action. As all views are heard, individuals find their common interests and are able to negotiate differences and come together, to "forge the intellectual and emotional partnership that would give each of us the energy and capacity for fresh growth and new challenges . . . an enhancement of each identity, through access to the other's broader experience" (Conway, 1994, p. 87).

The facilitator must keep the focus on the designated task and manage time well. He/she will monitor the time and energy expended for each session. Pacing the tasks will leave participants with a sense of optimism and energy. Some find it valuable to create a record of the group discussion so that all relevant insights can be retrieved, folded into later discussion, and created into a summary document.

When the school board of Tomball ISD, Tomball, Texas, wanted to improve its teamwork *and* its governance, the one-day workshop yielded the following report:

Workshop Summary

- Participants agreed that the purpose of a local school board is . . .
    . . . for local input and control of schools
    . . . to provide moral ownership of the district
    . . . to broker educational services for the owners
    . . . to ensure the best education possible using community resources
    . . . to perform as a sounding board and to share information with the community
- The trustees reviewed the governance policies Dr. Carr had created, following Carver's Policy Governance Model® and agreed to discuss them further at Tuesday evening board meetings.
- "John Carver reminds us that the board is to design the future, not mind the store!"
- The board discussed and defined their operational guidelines regarding: communication, time, executive sessions, and meeting evaluation.

Communication with Each Other

- Do's and don'ts in the meeting and in public were discussed.
- Manage constraints, such as being "on stage."
- Ways to better use public forums are presented.
- Ways to prevent, manage, and resolve conflict are discussed.
- We will have less staff talk and more board talk.

- We will listen with an open mind.
- We will listen to others as we would have them listen to us.
- We will make no assumptions about another's communications.
- We will recognize our individual talents and strengths.
- We will speak only when adding something new.
- Don't take "it" personally.
- We will write out important points to improve understanding (scripting).

Communication with Staff and Community

- We will continue to use the parent advisory council with more attendance by trustees to receive more public input.
- We will agree on the purpose and expected outcome for staff presentations at Monday meetings. After the presentations, we will ask questions of the staff, then dialogue with each other regarding the presentation/ program.
- Each trustee will share information about "their" school at the Tuesday evening meetings.

Time

In order to operate more efficiently and effectively, participants agreed to

- Be more efficient in trusteeship so we could focus on the education of our children.
- Proportion our time based on the mission/vision of Tomball ISD.

Executive Sessions

During executive sessions we will identify the real issue(s) and out intended outcome. We will try to remain unemotional. No personal attacks!

Current Issue

Dr. Carr provided an overview of the upcoming bond election and the differences in staff, board, and community members' roles in that bond election.

Meeting Evaluation

At the conclusion of each meeting, we will evaluate our performance using "blue slips." Summaries of these evaluations will be available at the next meeting and discussed.

The group feels that it rated about a 3 (on a 5-point scale) and all wished to create a board of trustees that was a 5+ + +!

This report of a *one-day workshop* demonstrates their ability to reflect on their interrelationships openly and honestly. It was one of the few times I've heard trustees consider ways to improve their behavior even when they are out of the public eye during executive sessions. It is always a joy to work with this board!

However, even the most skilled and knowledgeable facilitator can accomplish a limited amount in a one-day or weekend conference. In addition, short-term training unearths complaints and concerns without being able to resolve them. Because we are serious about improving the quality of school governance, boards and their supportive communities must participate in an ongoing program based on assessed needs and continuous feedback.

Because trustees say they want to make a difference in the education of their children, I believe it is imperative that those of us who provide board development programs provide them with the information, skills, and models to enable them to achieve their stated goals. We must teach boards more than how to mind the store; we must provide them with tools that will enable them to use their board time wisely and well.

With support and comprehensive training they can become knowledgeable, informed, and skilled in effective governance.

Better training of the governance team can support them as they adjust educational programs to the needs and aspirations of their citizens through goal setting, policy development, and resource allocation to encourage educational improvement for all students.

In summary, effective governing boards

- are clear about their role
- effectively carry out their responsibilities
- anticipate the consequences of their decisions
- balance competing and conflicting demands
- allocate scarce resources
- communicate appropriately with the public
- evaluate educational programs
- support educational reform

INTERACTIVE TRAINING STRATEGIES

Carousel Activity

For this activity selected questions are written at the top of flip-chart paper and taped to walls and doors about the room. (See examples below.) Divide the participants into the same number of groups as there are questions. Each group selects one scribe and stands by a chart. When the facilitator says "begin" they brainstorm answers to questions and write them down. In three minutes the facilitator tells each group to move clockwise around the room to the next chart. Rotate the groups until they are back at their original place. Have all be seated except for one reporter who briefly shares information from the charts.

The amount of information thus collected is richly abundant. It demonstrates very quickly the concept that many can generate more information than any individual could. The collected information provides material for much discussion through the workshop. If the charts are left up at the end of one day of training, they can be used the next day for participants to discuss, in clusters, what has been learned. Sample questions are

- What should a new trustee know about our district?

- What should a new trustee know about our board?
- What should the board know about the superintendent?
- The best part of being a school trustee is . . .
- What do school boards do?
- What does an individual member of a board need to know?
- Create an agenda for the orientation of novice trustees.
- List the qualities of an effective board member.
- In order for the board to be effective, all board members must . . .

Simulation Activities

At a cluster training or individual board workshops, simulation activities are valuable ways for trustees to see themselves and others in action. When they process the behaviors, it brings forth other issues and similar circumstances. With good facilitation, this reflection leads to healthy dialogue and, hopefully, improved communications during meetings.

Role plays are a fun way to experience some of the difficulties boards encounter in sharing information. Use eight volunteers to assume assigned roles as board members and the superintendent. The remainder observe, take notes, and provide feedback after the simulation.

Although simulations are interesting if trustees "play themselves," the participants may be more confortable (and entertaining) if the facilitator provides name tags for each participant, giving them a fake personality, or role that is not revealed for the others. For example, Sr. Lopez is concerned primarily about financial aspects of decisions; Dr. Rich is a strong supporter of anything new; Ms. Luis is an opponent of the superintendent. Such exaggerated characteristics provide opportunities to spotlight tendencies that improve or impede discussions among trustees.

The facilitator could provide the scenario first, then allow the board to work together to make the decision. Alternatively, let them act out the simulation, discuss the questions and answers, and then have them provide the ideal reaction by the board.

Prime the audience to be process observers. They are to observe who talks and who listens. Do all participate? They should notice unhelpful and helpful behaviors.

Sample Activities

Topic I: Year-Round Education

The task is for the board to make a decision regarding the superintendent's recommendation to implement year-round education (YRE). Assign each actor a position regarding YRE, as well as a statement regarding their communication style.

Topic II: To Train or Not to Train?

As an agenda item of the board, the board has been asked to consider and/or approve a local grant so the district can provide an innovative training program for women in non-traditional occupations (welder, truck driver, etc.).

What do they need to know to consider and/or approve such a grant? What information does the board need? What questions should the board ask? What would be the next step for the board to take?

BOARD SELF-EVALUATION

(1) Do we plan an annual workshop for our own self-evaluation and goal setting?   Yes_____ No_____
(2) *How* does the *board* evaluate itself?
(3) How do we provide for continuous improvement for the board?
(4) Does each trustee participate in professional activities (self-study, conferences, workshops) to improve its governance of the district's educational program?
                                        Yes_____ No_____
(5) What information do we need to improve our meetings?
(6) What information do we need to improve our relationships?

(*7*) What information do we need to improve our educational programs?

(*8*) What information do we need to improve our relationships with the community?

(*9*) What information do we need to improve our allocation of resources?

(*10*) What board development opportunities would be most efficient, effective, and economical for our assessed needs?

_____ Conference   _____ Print

_____ Cluster training   _____ Media

_____ Leadership team training _____ Interactive technology

(*11*) How do we provide opportunities for individual trustees to share information with other members of the leadership team?

(*12*) How do we evaluate our board development program?

CHAPTER 5

Overcoming the Social Challenges

WAITING for the board meeting to start, my neighbor and I were visiting. "Who makes the best trustee? Homemaker, company executive, former superintendent, or construction worker?"

He posed it as a multiple-choice question. My answer surprised him: "Yes! All of them! The best board is a mix of people, bringing diverse experiences and attitudes. It's the variations of gender, ethnicity, age, and education that provide the rich discussions that create the best solutions. If we didn't need such diversity, we wouldn't need boards at all."

At the same time, boards consisting of individuals that are too much alike or who have been together too long often fail to generate innovative ideas or represent their communities well. *Novice* trustees describe the *community*, and the *experienced* member describes the school district, i.e., number of children, rate of growth, percent of children on reduced lunch, etc., demonstrating how novice trustees are connected with *community* interests and experienced policy makers have become aligned with the educational program. Even though they are elected to represent the community, as they gain experience, trustees are more aligned with the superintendent than with their constituents.

There are many superintendents and boards working together for the good of the children. But, all too often, the reverse is true. Superintendents are usually pleased with a board that has been together for a long time. My experience is that trustees who have been together seven years or more think alike. Although the relationship is warm and supportive, there may be no progress in the educational system. They have become so similar that all but one could stay home!

The challenge is to overcome the inevitable group pressures to become a member of a productive team. By becoming aware of the strengths and weaknesses of group dynamics, they can develop the creative dynamics that result in the whole being larger than the sum of its parts.

THE BENEFITS OF TEAM LEADERSHIP

As the operation of educational institutions becomes continually more complex, the board of trustees and the superintendent must forge an intellectual and emotional partnership. For, as in any situation requiring multiple skills, experiences, and judgments, a team is preferable to a single individual. Full collaboration is essential to tranform limited resources and multiple political demands into a high-performing educational system.

Each trustee brings a wealth of knowledge and expertise to the board that others may not be aware of. Experience with management, insurance, curriculum design, law, construction, and education are all "gifts" that individuals bring to the decision-making body. Those trustees who are, or have been, educators count themselves especially fortunate, as they understand the educational jargon and milieu. One trustee was pleased with the composition of her board: an accountant, a president of a credit union, an owner of an auto dealership, a former math teacher, two Hispanic businessmen, and her own unique background. When the team has access to this expertise, it improves the team's effectiveness.

In addition to individual skills and experiences, each trustee represents a constituency with multiple needs and preferences. Although the needs of the neighborhood must be balanced with the needs of *all* children in the district, without all the pertinent information, decisions will be less accurate and commitment toward implementation diminished. All political realities must be taken into account.

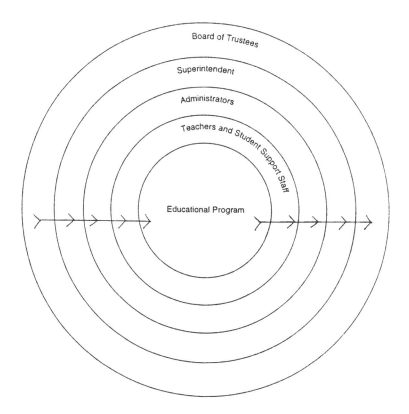

ORGANIZATIONAL CHART

CHARACTERISTICS OF EFFECTIVE BOARDS

Effective leadership teams demonstrate a sense of commitment to their collaborative work. These corporate bodies know that their work is to ensure the best education of the district's students within the available resources. Because advocating for students is their primary responsibility, they spend most of their time and energy working out educational issues. They have included the community in determining the district's goals and attaining them.

A foundation of trust and mutual respect is demonstrated by full participation of all members during meetings. They eagerly collaborate to use their collective wisdom. They see each other as resources, friends, and allies, rather than as enemies, competitors, or threats. They communicate with respect. The quality of their discussion reveals their preparation for the meeting.

Each trustee follows established procedures and processes for problem solving and decision making. They use their policies to guide their choices and understand the consequences of their decisions. When they need more information, they ask clarifying questions. They adhere to legal requirements regarding meetings and, of course, never share confidential information. They are not expected to achieve unanimity in all decisions, but there must be an agreement that once a decision has been made (whether by consensus, ballot, or voice vote) all will support the decision.

Because of continual change in the world of education and the complexities of board leadership, boards must provide for their own learning. Ironically enough, many school boards are reluctant to invest in their own growth, an issue that will be discussed in the next chapter. However, let us say here, that like athletes, to stay on the cutting edge you must be lifelong learners.

OVERCOMING INEVITABLE GROUP CHALLENGES

> With good evidence, many people believe that boards will always stumble from rubber stamping to meddling and back again. They believe the realities of group decision making forever destine boards to be incompetent groups of competent people.
>
> Carver (1991), p. xi

Overcoming "the realities of group decision making" requires conscious effort and skill from each trustee. The process of developing into a collegial group means each individual must maintain his/her own intellectual integrity within the pressures of the group. Whether in agreement or conflict, the pressure of the group may shape an individual's interpretation of speeches or influence voting patterns. For example, a trustee, in listening to discussion, may assume he is the only dissenter (or advocate) and vote contrary to his beliefs. We know, too, that in a group a single individual may advocate the adoption of more risky alternatives than when making solitary judgments, perhaps because of the ability to share responsibility.

Like any ongoing social system, the school board operates on the basis of shared values and expectations regarding acceptable behavior (Cistone, 1977). The novice will be guided and pushed (or hindered) to learn procedures, shared values, and expectations of the board. In a socialization process that takes days, months, or years, each individual adapts to the culture of the group. The process is an interactive one, with the group also being altered by the new member. If newcomers cannot adapt or accommodate to this powerful culture, they rebel or leave.

Success ranges from *assimilation* through *accommodation* to *rebellion*. If the culture of the board is powerful and the newcomer has a strong need to belong, he/she will become absorbed and *assimilated* into the group, effecting little change. Although incumbents and superintendent may prefer *assimilation* ("Don't make waves," "We've always done it this way"), *accommodation* is believed to be the ideal situation for continuous organizational improvement.

When the newcomer maintains his/her focus and personal goals while working within the group norms, the group benefits from new and (perhaps) creative perspectives. When the values and norms are a good fit for the novice, the newcomer will influence and be influenced by the existing board in a mutual adaptation process.

DEALING WITH OPPOSITION

Rebellion may occur when one member (or more) rejects the values and norms of the group. Sometimes a "renegade" has a personal ax to grind. Other times, the trustee may be thrust into rebelliousness by persons who share similar beliefs such as opposition to sex education or a tax hike.

When differences of opinion surface, communication may become actively confrontational. Because too much individualistic or idiosyncratic behavior can threaten the survival of a group, the board will attempt to manage the renegade's behavior. This dissonance brings an opportunity for all to learn new perspectives and rethink their own positions. Resolution of the conflict is awkward but necessary to avoid distress to participants, the educational staff, students, and community. Conflict is a necessary phase of group life, and group progress is unlikely if the leader cannot negotiate for resolution.

Without intervention, individuals may seek support and alliances for their own viewpoint, creating a hero, villain, or rescuer out of the superintendent or other trustees, creating even larger chasms of dissonance. If the poor behavior demonstrates lack of knowledge or skills, additional information or training may be helpful. In executive session or at a board retreat, the board president or external facilitator may provide information and redirection. If the behavior is inappropriate or illegal, peer pressure and sanctions may be necessary. Only if such interventions are not successful should the board make a public statement discrediting the behavior. (Because the superintendent is employed by the board, it is better if the superintendent is not involved.)

All too frequently, a board may split, and no matter what the issue, vote in factions. For example, on one occasion, four members of the board would vote for *only* one superintendent candidate, four more would vote for anyone *but* that candidate. Until the candidate officially withdrew, the board was unable to move forward. (Understandably, many superintendents refuse to move to a district where the board is not unanimous in its choice.) Such behaviors impede good governance.

Although boards are not expected to reach agreement in all matters, voting in a predictable pattern stalls the board's progress. If the executive belongs to one of the factions, the chair should point out that he/she is not a member of the board and encourage him/her to extricate himself from the situation. The trustees must discuss the real issue(s) that is (are) dividing the board and resolve it (them), perhaps in a board workshop with a trained facilitator/mediator. They must be reminded of the overriding importance of the district mission.

COHESIVE GROUPS

In homogenous communities, boards may have a stable history and accepted pattern of activity rendering them resistant to change. Trustees' relationships often pre-date their board status and they build on an already collegial relationship. Some boards represent only the community's power elite, not all the people. If the trustees have grown up together, sharing the same background and values, many of the complexities of group process are minimized and there is little observable conflict. A spirit of friendly rivalry or camaraderie exists within the board; trustees enjoy each other's company, even spending leisure time together.

However, although homogenous boards may be peaceful, they often fail to generate innovative ideas and may lack critical information to make informed decisions. If all the trustees have been together for more than five years, there is probably little debate or innovation. These cohesive groups risk becoming a "closed system," disallowing new information or persons into the group. Because they tend to readily agree with each other, they create the phenomenon known as "groupthink."

As trustees gain experience, they become more aligned with the educational environment than with their constituents. They are more reassured about the quality of teachers, the curriculum, and school discipline. Trustees with seven years of experience will talk like a superintendent about financial obligations, maintenance, and programs. Although superintendents are pleased with boards that stay together for many years, it is the disruptive tendencies of the novice that move an organization to explore new opportunities.

The tragic consequences of creating an illusion of unanimity and invulnerability have been thoroughly described by Halberstam (1969), Harvey (1988), Janis (1972), and McNamara (1995). To avoid the disadvantages of too much homogeneity, the board president may wish to designate a "provocateur" to critique each decision. By questioning assumptions and beliefs, trustees will be open to a greater number of alternatives.

CREATING HARMONY

The purpose of dialogue is to lower or remove the walls and barriers of misunderstanding that unduly separate us from each other. Individual differences must first be allowed to surface and be fought over so that the group can ultimately learn to accept, celebrate, and thereby transcend their differences. Confrontive, even angry, communication is sometimes necessary to focus on those barriers before they can be knocked down. When hidden agendas, assumptions, and conflicting interests are uncovered, a deeper level of communication is possible.

Knowing that teams benefit from a diversity of ideas, boards should discuss and agree on ways to manage conflicts *before* they arise. Open discussion that clarifies issues and expands the perspective of all participants contributes to mutual understanding. When communication is authentic, open disagreement and conflicts are *encouraged as constructive.* Competition gives way to cooperation and collaboration. Energy is channeled along more productive lines.

Just as jazz musicians give up their individual themes to "be in the groove," so trustees may need to relinquish their personal agendas and work together to resolve conflict. They can then negotiate a solution that points the district in a positive direction. Remembering their mission to provide the best education for *all* students, they seek ways to overcome their differences and achieve their common goals and priorities!

ETHICAL LEADERSHIP

- One trustee demonstrated ethical leadership when the district was about to build a new elementary school. He ran the only construction business in the area. Because there was no way there would not be a perception of a conflict of interest, he resigned his position.
- Another trustee was less ethical. He was up for re-election and didn't want to jeopardize his chance for success. He simply didn't show up when votes on controversial issues were taken!

This powerful, complex role requires persons of wisdom and demonstrated integrity, since the board has a great deal of influence and resources. Each trustee makes ethical decisions on a day-to-day basis. High personal standards and a sincere desire to work for the benefit of all the students support ethical behavior. Persons, groups, and agencies may pressure the trustee to allocate resources or make decisions biased in their favor. Managing those pressures requires decision-making skills, knowledge, and competencies.

Board leadership *must* be ethical. In fact, research shows that the public has higher expectations for members of the board than any other elected body (IEL, 1986). Therefore, the first task of the board should be to create its own code of ethics based on mutually agreed-upon values. Adopting and communicating such a code as part of its policy assists the board in monitoring its own behavior and provides a standard to reinforce such values in the daily operations of the district.

Trustees avoid many problems when they remember that no one member of the board has individual authority; it is the board as a whole that makes decisions. Placing the needs of *all* the students ahead of personal and political agendas is the cornerstone. In the same vein, once the board has voted, all must support the decision.

All trustees must demonstrate trust in and respect for others. Being prepared for meetings, attending them regularly, and working for effective communications between the board and the educational community are essential. Naturally all will avoid any perception of using the position for personal or professional gain. No single trustee should receive special favors or information from the superintendent.

COMMUNICATING WITH THE COMMUNITY

The school board seems to be alternately ignored and attacked by the public:

> The majority of the voting public, in my experience, do not care or have the time to get involved in the education of their children. Many

times I begged the public to get involved in issues only to be ignored until the decisions were made. Then and only then did people get involved. The board was more often than not lambasted by the very public that we asked for advice. We were continually criticized for not involving the teachers and public in decision making. No amount of pleading or prodding could get people involved.

Audience participation at most board meetings is three to four people. When discussing topics such as band and athletics, there is a house full.

Trustees, as servant-leaders, have a dual role. They represent the school administration's point of view to the community and ascertain and express the community's interests back to the leadership team. They must be on the outside—close to the ground. They should hear things, see things, know things, then carry that information back to the board.

Last May I was interviewed by a team and requested to serve on the board of directors. That's why my role is different, I must respond to my constituency; I must assume responsibility to these people and respond to certain goals that have been expressed to me.

School trustees celebrate opportunities to brag about their district and, more important, express their deep roots in the community: "I've lived here all my life," "My family has been here three to four generations." Their responses reveal not only their personalities and attitudes, but the values of the community. Often they are a long-term member of the community, even a former student of the district.

The superintendent is the outsider, the educational expert. In the faddish world of education, then, the superintendent moves for the latest educational strategy and the school board becomes the stable force. Paul Salmon, the late executive of American Association of School Administrators put it best: "Professionals must represent the professionally desirable; School boards must represent the politically possible."

Trustees are also on the inside, overseeing the superintendent and the success of the educational program. They must be well-informed in order to hold the administration accountable to the public. When they are successful, they gain the trust of their constituents, communicate their vision, and involve everyone in the process of change (Bennis, 1990).

One of the more difficult tasks for a sympathetic trustee is to acquire information from the community without usurping the administrative role: *"When I go out to talk about a problem, I create three more!"*

It is unrealistic to expect trustees not to be learning about the school through informal means. They are still members of the community, hearing things from their children, family members, and constituents. Ethical and conscientious trustees, however, must be careful not to make assumptions and jump to conclusions without more information. A high number of complaints from parents and community members may indicate problems in relationships *or* an empowered community that has found its voice and articulates high expectations!

Peruse your board policies regarding trustee and board communication with the public. Pay special attention to policies regarding grievance processes and procedures and follow them! Adhering faithfully to those policies will promote confidence and trust in the educational community as well as the integrity of the board.

With other trustees, develop ways to keep communication open, such as expanding the use of public forums on specific programs as well as budget hearings. In larger communities, boards have had success meeting at each campus on a rotating basis, touring the building, and hosting a reception prior to the meeting. Some boards designate each of their members to be their eyes and ears on a single campus, allowing for a wide range of information. The trustee attends meetings and celebrations on that campus and reports back to the entire board. You visit campuses only as a parent or citizen, not building inspector, since maintenance is an administrative function.

Because you are perceived as an expert with unrealistic powers and abilities, you must remind citizens that you are only one-fifth/seventh/ninth of the vote. Never divulge privileged information or promise what you cannot deliver. In order not to impede the orderly process of staff evaluations, you should be generally supportive and positive of them in public. Your enthusiasm about programs might encourage other citizens to become more involved with the educational program.

COMMUNICATING WITH STAFF

What's wrong with this picture?

The primary staff were angry with the new assistant principal, so they invited the trustees to a meeting. (The principal was aware of the meeting, but not the superintendent or the assistant principal.) Four of the seven trustees attended and listened to the complaints of the staff.

- Trustees forgot they have no power outside of a duly constituted board meeting and agreed, by attending the meeting, to listen to grievances outside the chain of command, compromising the grievance process.
- The staff should have discussed their grievance up the chain of command: the principal, area superintendent, superintendent. Only after exhausing all other remedies would they have petitioned the board at a legally constituted meeting, following board grievance policies.
- Each trustee should have individually declined the offer to attend such an off-the-record meeting and informed the superintendent of the situation immediately.
- The meeting was illegal, since a majority of the board attended a meeting that was not legally posted.

Trustees who are unclear about their role may believe their job is to become advocates for the staff. However, once the trustee assumes the role of chaplain, detective, building contractor, or liaison to staff, he/she has lost the ability to set policy, evaluate programs, ensure accountability, and serve as a member of the appeal board in an impartial hearing, if such a step becomes necessary.

When approached by a staff member with a concern, trustees

should remind the staff member of the chain of command and the fact that no single individual has authority. Because *all* the information must be known by the *entire* board before they make a decision, a single trustee should *never* become the spokesperson for the staff.

When you remind citizens to follow the chain of command, you improve communication. When you insist that responsible parties talk to each other, you support good management and keep yourself from becoming a lightning rod for incessant complainers! If you find you are receiving more complaints than other trustees, visit with the board president about ways to redirect them.

Persons tend to complain to the person judged most likely to listen, instead of going to the responsible party(ies). In addition, there may be more to the story. A campus with an unusual amount of staff complaints, transfer requests, or attrition may signal poor leadership *or* it may be the result of a principal whose high standards have met staff resistance! Trustees must notify the superintendent and board president of critical concerns and work together to resolve repeated and ongoing complaints.

All trustees who are parents of students in the district must learn to manage the challenges of wearing two hats. Although you know that visiting your child's school as a parent does not entitle you to special privileges or opportunities, some teachers may be intimidated. Many trustees send the other parent to participate in teacher conferences or to deal with parent-teacher-student issues so as not to blur their roles. It seems to be one of the sacrifices trustees make.

Most boards agree that requests for information from staff must come from the board as a whole, through the superintendent.

COMMUNICATING WITH THE MEDIA

Although some districts have a public relations department, the entire leadership team must accept their role as advocates for the district. Following board policy regarding interactions with the media, trustees should create and maintain a positive relationship with reporters. In order to enable the press to report successes of the district and its students, the media should be provided information about upcoming events, and information concerning employees, programs, and awards. They should have a copy of the board agenda packet, similar to those received by the trustees.

Some boards select a single spokesperson, especially to report on controversial issues; others encourage trustees to accept any opportunity to be a positive influence on behalf of the district. Remember that even when you wish to speak as a private citizen, you will be perceived as speaking for the board. When speaking in a public setting, the following general guidelines may be helpful:

- Stick to the facts.
- Use prepared statements to prevent being led offtrack or misquoted.
- Make your answer brief and direct, avoiding educational jargon.
- When there is a reason that you cannot respond, such as pending litigation, board policy, or lack of information, never say "no comment"—tell why you cannot answer or give the names of someone else who can.

BOARD SELF-EVALUATION

Building Trust

(1) Do we know and recognize the talents and experience each trustee brings to the board?   Yes____ No____
(2) Do we create opportunities to know each other better and determine our common values?   Yes____ No____
(3) Do we demonstrate respect for each other?
                                                           Yes____ No____

Communication

(4) Has the board adopted policies for trustee communication . . .

- with staff?   Yes_____ No_____
- with community members?   Yes_____ No_____
- with the media?   Yes_____ No_____

(5) Do all trustees know and follow the policies?
                                           Yes_____ No_____

Ethical Behavior

(6) Has the board created and adopted its own code of ethics?
                                           Yes_____ No_____

(7) Does each trustee follow the board's code of ethics?
                                           Yes_____ No_____

(8) Does each trustee understand his/her personal responsibility in following the code and bring credit to the board at all times?   Yes_____ No_____

CHAPTER 6

Working in Harmony

The world is crying out for leadership. In both the crises that affect the future of the globe and the urgent everyday issues that confront every family and village, the time is at hand to pause, to step back and ask ourselves, "What is leadership and what is expected of us as leaders?"

Terry (1993), p. xvi

BOARDS AND SUPERINTENDENTS AS EDUCATIONAL LEADERS

AS the operation of educational institutions becomes continually more complex, skillful leadership and cooperation of the board of trustees and the superintendent are essential for success. They must work together to establish the vision for the district and drive the district toward excellence. To effectively meet the challenges of public education, school boards and superintendents must function together as a leadership team with complementary roles.

Effective leadership teams have clarified the board's job, the executive's job, and the link between them. But, as numerous dissertations have confirmed, defining the separate roles is probably the biggest stumbling block in building harmonious relationships. Although state law often delineates duties for the superintendent and board, local custom has blurred many boundaries. Is it the discussion or is it a collaborative effort? Should the board pressure the superintendent to select a favorite principal for a central office position? Who hires the athletic director? Does board membership entitle positions to a given number of relatives?

Images may be helpful here. Brickell and Paul (1988) use a clock to illustrate the goal-setting and evaluation modes: twelve to three o'clock for goal and policy setting and nine to twelve o'clock for the evaluation mode. The administration deals with the lower half of the clock (three to nine o'clock). Another model uses two mountain tops (goals and vision) with a valley of administrative work between. Both the board and the superintendent must adhere to their respective roles and responsibilities. Clearly differentiating the roles establishes the balance of power.

This balance of power is essential, since both the board and the superintendent must be capable and powerful in order to build a dynamic, high-performing team. The superintendent and board must see each other as equals. Boards that select weak superintendents and superintendents who disable their boards make their own jobs more difficult.

The relationship between the superintendent and the board must be supportive to create a climate for success. Each member of the leadership team must act responsibly and encourage others to do so. A board and superintendent behaving like rude children instead of adult leaders bring no glory to the district.

Because the superintendent is the primary contact for information regarding the complexities of education, he/she must encourage and support novice trustees as they learn the ropes. Providing policy manuals, background information, and resources for each trustee enables them to become part of a "competent community." With the board president, determine ways to assess board development needs and create agendas that focus on policy-making, planning, and evaluation of educational programs.

SEEKING THE IDEAL SUPERINTENDENT

An outstanding superintendent in a low-income area in the

Texas Valley gained attention when he led his district through a school bus tragedy. His calm presence and reassuring words led the community through its grief. [Former] Supt. Ralph Cantu has a quiet, self-assured leadership style that combines pressure and support to motivate students and staff. He developed one of the highest performing districts in the state of Texas. The quality of trust and respect between him and his board is almost palpable. He retires soon. What will his successor be like?

Second only to its powerful role as policymaker is the importance of making a wise selection for the CEO of the district: the superintendent. Effective boards hire the superintendent they feel is the most able to guide the district toward excellence.

Because research demonstrates again and again that the success of any community, whether a business enterprise, non-profit organization, or school district is closely dependent on the skills of its leader, the board faces their greatest challenge when selecting a new superintendent. Whether they carry out the search themselves or seek outside consultants for support, the plethora of books, programs, and definitions of leadership offers scant help, for finding the best leader seems to be as difficult as finding a life-partner. Over and above the extensive lists of credits, publications, and years of experience each candidate brings to the position, the chemistry has to be just right!

> "Our last superintendent was a good instructional leader," the board president declared, "but he didn't mix well in the community. When we interviewed for this superintendent, we wanted someone who would fit in. When Supt. Jones first came, he walked up and down the main street and introduced himself to everyone!"

An effective board will begin the search process by doing some serious self-study to determine what qualities and experience they seek. Then they can determine if the right person is already available within the current staff. If so, then they can carry on with a minimum of interruption and save the district the expense of hiring an external consultant and the suspense of waiting for new leadership. If not, they must decide if they are competent and capable of searching for a superintendent themselves or whether they wish to hire a consultant. Either way, the board must decide the qualities and abilities that are essential, then select the one individual who best matches those requirements.

> "How do you make certain that the candidate is a Christian?" a trustee asked me during a workshop.
>
> MR: "What qualities, exactly, are you seeking? Regular attendance at choir practice and Sunday Services?" "Oh no," he responded, "I want my superintendent to be honest and trustworthy. A role model for the children in the district."
>
> "Ah, well, then those are the qualities you need to seek. Do not confuse labels with qualities."

Most boards expect the superintendent to work closely with the board and community to establish high academic goals for all students and select and motivate the staff to implement the educational program.

The superintendent is expected to be the professional consultant regarding educational programs, legal issues, technology, budget, staffing, and facilities. Even though the superintendent may not be directly involved with the students, he or she must be the leader of the educational program. Responsibilities such as public relations, personnel decisions, staff development, transportation, etc., are delegated to staff in larger districts but are the superintendent's responsibility in smaller districts. Even when the responsibilities are delegated, it is still the leader's job to ensure success.

When a board selects a superintendent, they are selecting an administrator, a person to be the CEO, the Chief Executive Officer of the district. This leader then articulates a vision for the district and empowers others to implement the vision. Personal qualities of honesty, integrity, and respect for diversity are essential. The board may wish to create or review an inventory of skills and knowledge, such as those listed by the *AASA* (1993) publication *Professional Standards for the Superintendency*.

Perhaps your board will consider the following questions and add some of their own to help focus the search.

Personal Qualities

- What qualities do we, as a board, value in a leader?
- What leadership style will be most effective in working with our staff?
- What competencies are essential for effective leadership in our district?
- Are the candidate's answers so forthright, direct, courageous, and credible that we know we will be able to trust this person?

Instructional Leadership Qualities

- What leadership is essential in order to implement our district's strategic plan?
- What background must our superintendent have in school improvement and instructional management?
- Will this individual, as superintendent, implement curriculum decisions based on personal preferences or district needs?
- Is this leader committed to shared decision making at the campus level?
- Is this leader a change agent? What innovations has he or she implemented previously and to what effect?

Management of Human and Financial Resources

- In what way will this leader use both human and financial resources to support our academic goals and our communities' values?
- How do we know that the superintendent will be effective in securing and retaining staff?
- What will we expect regarding recommendations for new staff positions and personnel?
- What demonstrated experience does the candidate have regarding prudent administration of resources?

Student Management

- What ideas does this leader have regarding student management?
- What ideas does this leader have regarding alternative schools?
- Is this person knowledgeable about legal issues regarding students?

Board/Superintendent Relationships

- What kind of relationship do we wish to have with the new superintendent?
- Will this person be formal or informal in communicating with us? Will our communication styles be compatible?
- What will our board meetings be like?

Experience and Professional Development

- Does the candidate have the necessary experience to lead our district?
- What academic background must we have for our superintendent? Is an earned Ph.D. essential or will a combination of academic and on-the-job training be suitable?
- Do we want a leader who has experience with all levels of education? Does he or she have such experience?
- If there are deficits in the resume (i.e., an unfinished dissertation) or skill deficits (weak public speaking skills, for example), could we support professional development to remedy the deficits?
- Will professional and social affiliations on local and national boards add value to our district or detract from necessary leadership here?

Community Relationships

- Will our superintendent be an effective communicator with all the publics involved: internal staff, school trustees, parents, businesses, the religious community, and students?
- What formal and informal activities do we expect of our number one public relations officer?
- In what way will this candidate create and maintain excellent relationships with the community?
- If the superintendent is expected to communicate with civic groups regularly, will he or she be comfortable with that?

Consider the need to match leadership styles with the socio-political needs of the community. Will the community do better with a dynamic showman or a peacemaker? A revolutionary change-agent or moderate one? An autocrat or a coalition builder? A quiet, behind-the-scenes motivator might have a hard time encouraging a fixed-income community to pass bond issues, but might be a good fit for a community with an already excellent academic program and strong community support. Although a flashy "city-slicker" may never be accepted in a quiet, rural community, those political skills are essential for superintendents to flourish (survive?) in urban districts. Hire a dynamic, charismatic, externally focused superintendent only if there is a hard-working staff willing to carry out the day-to-day duties of running the district.

Trade-offs

Even the best superintendents will not possess every desired quality. Perhaps a trade-off will benefit everyone. If the superintendent is not comfortable in public speaking, are there other administrators who could carry those responsibilities? If you want a superintendent with an informal style, but the best candidate for the educational program wears three-piece suits *always,* will you relinquish your personal wishes for the best educational leader? Decide what the non-negotiables are and what compromises you can make! Although you are hiring skills and experience, it is in the details and style that difficulties often occur. Because the personal style of the superintendent probably won't change, pay attention to the chemistry and fit!

Learning More about Candidates

It is amazing to me that boards continue to hire superintendents who bankrupt one district after another, have a poor track record of academic success, are known to have a less-than-exemplary personal life, or who create conflict everywhere. Although strict personnel laws and the threat of litigation make it difficult to acquire some information, and some folks have been known to fudge recommendations just to get a weak administrator out of the district, there are ways to get facts about the candidate.

Call the local papers in the candidate's current and former communities. Ask for clippings regarding the schools, school board meetings, and related issues during the time the candidate served that community. Even taking into account the newspaper's or reporter's bias and political climate of the community, you may learn a great deal about the individual's political skills.

If the candidate is currently a superintendent, ask the board president of his/her current district about board policies unique to the district and/or adopted while the superintendent served there. (A new policy limiting the superintendent's ability to leave the district without specific board permission is *not* a good sign!) Board agendas and minutes will give you a preview of your future board meetings under this leader. What lawsuits are pending against the district? What role did the superintendent play in attempts to resolve the issues before the lawsuits were filed?

Of course you will check out the district's test data. How did students *such as yours* fare under this academic leader? Take into account that new programs usually take three to five years to show results. Startling success may be attributed to a new curriculum, better trained staff, or "teaching to the test." *Where does the candidate place the credit?*

Hiring an effective superintendent and maintaining a mutually respectful relationship are the most important tasks for any board. Time, resources, and energy spent in making a wise decision will pay off in staff and student performance for years to come. Then build a relationship that will last beyond the honeymoon with trust and authentic communication.

Relationship Building

Although it is often said that the most imnportant task of a board is the choice of chief executive, the establishment of an effective relationship is even more important. Research and experience indicate that dissonance within the leadership team is created by narrow agendas, mistrust, and special treatment for selected individuals. Breakdowns in communcation and failing to focus on the educational program also cause dissension. When all members of the team agree on and follow their own operating procedures they prevent misunderstandings. Productive boards demonstrate respect, ethical behavior, open and honest communication, role clarity, and political skills.

Trust is essential in building a leadership team. Indeed, problems in the superintendent and board relationship are more often caused by inequitable treatment and lack of openness than technical incompetence. If a superintendent withholds information or some trustees get special treatment, the delicate balance is upset. Embarrassing any member of the team is bound to have negative consequences, whether it occurs as a rude question at a board meeting or a statement in public. Once trust is lost, it is seldom regained (Canada, 1989).

Effective leadership teams communicate frequently, making and keeping agreements. They are patient with each other, remembering that building trust takes time. There *will* be disappointment and setbacks. All trustees must place district needs above personal interests. Time, energy, and resources must focus on students and educational outcomes. All meetings then focus on those common goals.

Boards and superintendents must become like a jazz ensemble, continually evolving new music with diverse talents, unlikely instruments, and fluid melodies. But just as with any musical group, there is order, rhythm, and balance. They are interdependent, trusting each other to perform his/her part well. The musicians must agree on the key, the timing, and leadership. Dissonance is expected, but it eventually resolves.

SUPERINTENDENT EVALUATION

During the annual superintendent evaluation process, the board and superintendent should agree on specific goals and expectations that support the strategic and campus plans. During the process, the trustees and the superintendent identify ways the board helped or hindered the superintendent in accomplishing these designated goals.

The board of Lovelady ISD in East Texas demonstrated well the interrelationship of the board and superintendent when they created these goals for themselves and the superintendent.

Nine Goals for the Lovelady ISD Leadership Team

Area I: Administration and School Climate

- Our goal for the superintendent in this area is to promote positive staff relations so that the board is known as supportive/part of the team.
- We, as a board, will support the superintendent in implementing this goal by projecting a supportive attitude to staff and encouraging the superintendent to invite staff and students, etc. to board meetings to share successes.

Area II: School Improvement

- Our goal for the superintendent in this area is with the staff and community, etc. to develop goals and objectives for the district.

- We, as a board, will support the superintendent in implementing this goal by selecting a qualified superintendent, providing a clear role description, goals, objectives, and regular feedback.

Area III: Instructional Management

- Our goal for the superintendent in this area is to provide information regarding student performance through data collection, one-on-one discussions with staff members, and surveying the attitude of staff and students. Staff development will be based on student data, administration and staff input, and district goals.
- We, as a board, will support the superintendent in implementing this goal by providing time and money and recognizing and celebrating staff.

Area IV: Personnel Management

- Our goal for the superintendent in this area is to maintain stability of our staff.
- Our goal for the superintendent in this area is to assist principals in assessing and documenting personnel to improve staff performance.
- We, as a board, will support the superintendent in implementing this goal by staff incentives and benefits and providing for staff development opportunities.

Area V: Administration and Fiscal/Facilities Management

- Our goal for the superintendent in this area is to keep a preventive facilities maintenance program in place.
- Our goal for the superintendent in this area is to anticipate needs so the board can budget accordingly.
- Our goal for the superintendent in this area is to work with

the board in developing a budget based on district's needs and goals.
- We, as a board, will support the superintendent in implementing this goal by funding the maintenance needs.

Area VI: Student Management

- Our goal for the superintendent in this area is to work with the principals to ensure a wholesome, safe, learning environment.
- We, as a board, will support the superintendent in implementing this goal by reviewing, updating, and ensuring uniform implementation of student policies.

Area VII: Board/Superintendent Relations

- Our goal for the superintendent in this area is to respect each other's roles and responsibilities.
- We, as a board, will support the superintendent in implementing this goal by developing a systematic evaluation process for the superintendent.
- Our goal for the superintendent in this area is to maintain clear, honest, and open communication.
- We, as a board, will support the superintendent in implementing this goal by continuing our own board development.

Area VIII: Professional Growth and Development

- Our goal for the superintendent in this area is that he will attend professional development opportunities and report to the board.
- Our goal for the superintendent in this area is to keep the board informed about professional development events prior to attendance.
- We, as a board, will support the superintendent in implementing this goal by providing resources.

Area IX: School/Community Relations

- Our goal for the superintendent in this area is to continue to inform the community about the district through the calendar and newsletter; he will maintain high visibility within the community and conduct a community survey.
- We, as a board, will support the supperintendent in implementing this goal by being well-informed and accepting responsibility.

Because the goals were clear and the board was committed to the superintendent's success, the goals were accomplished. The superintendent received a salary increase and additional support for his programs.

WHAT SHOULD A SUPERINTENDENT EXPECT OF THE BOARD?

Many a superintendent has felt about a board the way the Quaker spinster did about a husband: it takes a very good one to be better than none.

Superintendents usually want their board to look at the big picture and avoid narrow agendas. They expect the board to identify problems and issues, not solutions. They expect the board to be clear about their expectations, then delegate the authority and responsibility to administer the school district and implement the district's plan.

The superintendent will expect trustees to channel administrative questions, concerns, and problems through him or her so answers can be researched appropriately, rather than come as a surprise at board meetings. Trustees don't surprise the superintendent at board meetings but communicate concerns and questions as they surface.

Superintendents value the board's ability to act as a buffer between the community and the educational system, channeling administrative questions and problems through him or her. Trustees respect the administrator's time, not using him as a "go-fer" or meeting for weekly luncheon dates. And, of course, the board provides the necessary resources, including an adequate salary, to accomplish the district's goals.

Such highly visible community and educational leaders have an obligation to follow district policies and behave cordially to one another at all times! In order for every board meeting to be conducted thoughtfully and purposefully, successful boards list their operating values and expectations. Here is a starter list:

- Everyone clearly understands the district's mission and works with other members of the board to implement that mission.
- All are advocates for student success and carry out duties and responsibilities as a team effort.
- Everyone knows his/her role and the role and responsibilities of others.
- Every member attends all meetings, unless there is an unexpected emergency and he/she has been excused! When unable to fulfill obligations, it is appropriate for the trustee to resign.
- Each follows agreed-upon procedures in placing items on the agenda. NO exceptions and NO surprises!
- Offer suggestions, comments, ideas, and information in a helpful manner.
- Share information readily; everyone participates and communicates clearly, directly, and to the point.
- If voting against a motion, tell why *prior* to the vote.
- Cooperate in implementing the decision (even if you voted against it!).
- Follow adopted policies or amend them if needed.
- Continually evaluate all procedures, practices, and policies.
- Focus on cooperation rather than competition.
- Show respect for varying viewpoints.
- Collaborate to serve the needs of the board and district.

Boards that build trust and support have become a true community. They have learned how to manage relations with each other and the larger society and can cope with the problems of its collective life. They agree on their guiding values and clearly communicate and follow them. Those values are then integrated into the board's activities: setting policies, establishing goals, allocating resources, gathering and communicating information, monitoring performance, and advocating for the best educational opportunities.

An allegory representing such a supportive relationship was included by Ben Canada (1989), Superintendent of the Atlanta City School System, in his dissertation:

> Once upon a time a man asked the Angel Gabriel the difference between heaven and hell. The Angel said, "Come, it would be easy to show you."
>
> He took him into a large room where many starving people sat around a large table that had a large pot of soup in the middle. Everyone had spoons, but the handles were too long for any one person to feed himself. The people looked miserable. "That," said the Angel, "Is hell!"
>
> Then he took the man into another large room where there were more people sitting around a similar table with a similar pot of soup in the center. Here, however, everyone was plump and happy.
>
> "That is heaven," said Gabriel.
>
> "Why were the people so satisfied there?" asked the man.
>
> "Here," he said, "they have learned to feed each other."

WORKING IN HARMONY

Workshop for the Leadership Team: Proposed Agenda

Objectives

When this workshop is complete, the leadership team will

- improve their working relationships
- provide long-term vision for the district
- clarify and discriminate the roles of the superintendent and the board

- describe ways they will improve the governance of the district
- focus time and energy on educational outcomes
- evaluate educational outcomes based on measurable criteria

Awareness/Needs Assessment

- carousel activity and discussion

Working in Harmony

- developing trust
- ethical behavior
- the advantages and challenges of team leadership
- communicating with the community
- the ideal board meeting
- nominations for board of the year

Roles, Responsibilities, and Relationships

- review the policies regarding board and superintendent responsibilities; compare and contrast roles
- sunshine laws and effective meetings

Working with Staff and Community

- review district's goals
- review policies regarding complaints and grievances
- roles and expectations in implementing site-based decision making

The Education Program

- What's happening in the district?
- What do we want for our students?
- How do we make it happen?
- determining next steps
- closure and evaluation

BOARD SELF-EVALUATION

Learning and Improving our Roles and Relationships

(*1*) Has the board established an effective, ongoing evaluation process for the superintendent?   Yes_____ No_____

(*2*) Do all trustees understand the goals and role of the board?
          Yes_____ No_____

(*3*) Do all trustees know who is and who should be doing what?
          Yes_____ No_____

(*4*) How do we plan to improve our working relationships?

A great unifying and focusing activity is to allow each trustee to complete the following assignment. As they read their statement aloud, they make a commitment to the creation of an outstanding governance team.

Nomination Form for Outstanding School Board, 199?–199?

Let's pretend that you have been a member of the board for at least four years, working closely with other members of your leadership team to improve the quality of education in your district. The superintendent wishes to nominate your board as the outstanding school board for your state.

What do you want your superintendent to say about your board? Write out the key points.

What will *you* do the next four years to make such a nomination possible?

CHAPTER 7

Meetings That Matter

Sir, we concern ourselves at Board meetings with bursted boilers. Whether the custodian can be asked to use the gang mower on the football field, that kind of thing. We don't get into educational matters near as much as some people think.

John Hersey

URBAN boards work in a fishbowl, with reporters, TV cameras, and large audiences; the boards of smaller districts meet in a small room around a conference table, signing checks and taking care of business in a less formal matter. Some boards meet about 5:30 P.M. and are finished by 8:00 P.M.; the atmosphere is pleasant and the board quickly moves through the agenda. Others begin at 7:00, recess into executive session, return much later, and carry on to the wee hours. Some meetings are tense and angry; others are routine and perfunctory with a curious, supportive, or distressed audience.

Unfortunately, most board meetings are tedious, dull, and a waste of time for the leadership team and the audience. Judging by agendas of districts of all sizes, board business is mostly buildings and grounds, maintenance, and budget amendments. In other words, no matter how intense the rhetoric is about keeping up with technology, Goals 2000, preparing for the 21st century, etc., board meetings are still about "bursted boilers."

MEETING PREPARATION

Knowing how to spend one's time in ways that increase, rather than reduce, the chances of realizing one's vision separates strong leaders from their less fortunate colleagues.

Duke (1987)

Trustees say they want to make a difference for kids. However, by law, the board can discuss only those items that are on the agenda; if educational programs ("kids") are not on the agenda, they won't be discussed. Therefore, the person(s) who sets the agenda determines the work of the board. So, if most of what your board does either does not need to be done or is a waste of time when done by the board, change the agenda. Determine ways to have it more nearly reflect the district's goals.

Who sets the agenda? The superintendent does, in consultation with the board president. It has been my experience that administrators are very selective about the items they place on the agenda. One superintendent said he never asked the board a question unless he knew the answer was yes. Implicit in that statement is his intention to persuade individual trustees to vote *in favor* of an item prior to discussion at the meeting. Although curricular decisions seldom are brought before the board, some administrators place certain items on the agenda so the board will share in the responsibility when controversy erupts.

Items for the agenda may be contributed by any trustee or member of the community. The board-adopted policy detailing the agenda preparation must be available to trustees, educators, and the public. A form such as shown in Figure 7.1 and used by the school board of Moscow, Idaho, might be useful. Although many boards need only a simple written request before the agenda is posted, this more formal procedure allows for concerns to be recorded.

Careful planning makes the best use of the collective wisdom of the trustees. Creating conditions for efficient and productive meetings is also good for public relations and the educational system. About a week prior to the meetings, the board president works with the superintendent to organize the agenda items. Because tedious agendas encourage boards to focus on micro-

```
┌─────────────────────────────────────────────────────────────────┐
│              REQUEST TO BE PLACED ON THE AGENDA                   │
│                           OF THE                                  │
│              MOSCOW, IDAHO, SCHOOL BOARD AGENDA                    │
│                                                                   │
│  To:          Board of Trustees                                   │
│  From:                                                            │
│  Subject:                                                         │
│                                                                   │
│  Background Information:                                          │
│                                                                   │
│                                                                   │
│                                                                   │
│                                                                   │
│  Rationale for Request:                                           │
│                                                                   │
│                                                                   │
│                                                                   │
│                                                                   │
│  Administrative Recommendations:                                  │
│                                                                   │
│                                                                   │
│                                                                   │
│                                                                   │
│  Financial Implications:                                          │
│                                                                   │
│                                                                   │
│                                                                   │
│  Placed on the Agenda of the Board of Trustees on _____ (Date)│
└─────────────────────────────────────────────────────────────────┘
```

Figure 7.1. Sample Form.

management instead of long-term goals, the agenda must be created so that the majority of the time is spent discussing educational issues: curriculum, staff, and the district's students.

First, eliminate any items that do not require board discussion or approval; information items should not be on the agenda at all! Clustering routine items on a consent agenda shows respect for the time and energy of the board. Some allocate a set amount of time for each discussion as a way to monitor the use of time. The board then agrees to adhere to the time constraint or negotiate for new limits.

Consider the items that are expected to generate discussion. Some topics may be divisive; others may need creative energy. Place strategic, crucial, or difficult issues near the beginning of the meeting to allow for thoughtful deliberation and dialogue. Others are fairly routine but need some discussion before the vote. The public appreciates the courtesy of having controversial items placed early, so they can leave before the executive session and routine business. Take such considerations into account when determining the order of the meeting.

THE BOARD PRESIDENT

In addition to collaborating with the superintendent to create an educationally-focused agenda, skilled board presidents provide an environment for effective and productive board meetings. They ensure that the board has adopted and follows standard rules of order and legal guidelines. The president may also encourage preliminary board committee sessions and trustee preparation to streamline the stated meeting. The board president must demonstrate skill in meeting management, communicating with the public, and working with the superintendent.

Because groups work best when they have selected their own leader, the board as a whole should elect its president at the first regular board meeting following election or appointment of trustees. This selection should be based on demonstrated leadership skills, *not* a return for favors, or seniority.

Trustees might consider the following questions before selecting an individual for this crucial role. Will this person, as board president . . .

- Provide leadership for the board?
- Work with the superintendent to provide for the orientation of each novice trustee in a timely manner?
- Work with the superintendent to create an agenda that is focused on educational needs of the district?
- Model legal and ethical behavior at all times?
- Manage all meetings well, following board-adopted policies and parliamentary procedures?
- Ensure that all meetings, including executive sessions, adhere to legal requirements?
- Maintain control of board meetings, ensuring and supporting purposeful dialogue on non-routine matters?
- Ensure that the district-adopted policies are current, followed, and available to trustees, educational staff, and the public?
- Provide for a successful two-way communication process with the community?

PUBLIC INPUT

Gathering information is crucial to success as a policymaker. Without enough information, the board is dependent on the superintendent, conventional wisdom, or public pressure. It must provide a forum at board meetings for constituents to share their needs and expectations. This enables all information to be heard by the entire corporate body.

Although the board meets in public, it is *not* a public meeting. The board must conduct its business without interruption. Create and follow a policy that allows for community input at selected times during the meeting. Usually, those who wish to speak are asked to sign up before the meeting, so they can be called on in order. Some boards provide two opportunities, allowing citizens to speak at the beginning of the meeting about agenda items and at the end about board actions. Allowing persons to speak before each vote is unnecessary and quickly gets out of hand. It is essential that whatever procedure the board adopts into policy be held to *consistently.*

The local board of Lockhart ISD provides a leaflet (Figure 7.2) welcoming all guests, describing the purpose and responsibilities of the local school board and the sources of board authority. It is a pleasant symbol of the "openness" of this board and provides important information for the public, along with the form to request time to address the board.

A celebration by students at the beginning of each board meeting sets the tone and encourages an audience. After the awards, ceremonies, and celebrations, most boards provide an opportunity for the public to share its concerns. At the beginning of the public forum, the president should remind the audience that the board, by law, will hear, but not discuss or act on, an item not on the agenda. Remind the audience of the time limit and request speakers to address all comments to the chair.

A three- or five-minute time limit for speakers is usually sufficient. When many are to speak on the same topic, they should select a spokesperson. If there are many speakers and/or a controversial topic, a public forum may be more appropriate than a regular business meeting of the board.

Following a presentation, the president may state the board's policy related to the area of concern, especially if the speaker (delegation) is not aware of, or has not followed, the chain of command. The president may refer complaints to the superintendent or request the speaker to put the complaint in writing to ensure that it's being dealt with appropriately. Whether by staff intervention or a future board agenda item, all concerns should be noted and remedied, if possible.

Because the public often is unaware of the grievance process or how to resolve issues through the chain of command, the board may listen to a disproportionate number of angry people. Although it is always difficult to listen to angry speakers, the benefits are great, since angry people who are heard often

LOCKHART ISD PUBLIC INFORMATION FORM
THE BOARD OF EDUCATION
WELCOMES YOU

THE PURPOSE of this booklet is to acquaint you with board procedures and to make your visit more informative and worthwhile.

BOARD MEETINGS are open to the public and minutes of meetings are available upon request.

WE HOPE that you will attend often.

THE AMERICAN WAY. . .

LOCAL CONTROL of the Lockhart Schools through a board of education elected by our citizens is part of the American way of life. This keeps our public schools responsive to the popular will and helps to give this nation a system of education unmatched by any other country at any time.

THE BOARD'S seven members are elected by the qualified voters of the school district. The members, who serve without pay, choose their own officers.

THE BOARD'S major responsibilities are:

- To set the policies for the **LOCKHART PUBLIC SCHOOLS**
- To develop and improve the educational program
- To secure adequate financing
- To maintain an efficient school plant
- To choose the chief executive (the superintendent of schools)
- To provide qualified personnel
- To maintain good community relations

SOURCES OF BOARD AUTHORITY

THE TEXAS LEGISLATURE empowers the board of education to manage the free public schools. The board has authority to exercise the right of eminent domain in acquiring property for the public schools.

THE BOARD conducts the school program in accordance with the state constitution and the standards set by the Texas Education Agency. The board carries out all educational functions not specifically delegated to the Texas Education Agency by the state legislature.

Figure 7.2.

THE BOARD is a policy-making body. It delegates the general administration of the school district to a professional administrative staff headed by the superintendent of schools.

PRIOR TO THE REGULAR MEETINGS OF THE BOARD — normally the third Tuesday night of each month — the administration prepares an agenda listing those matters requested by trustees and/or the superintendent of schools.

SCHOOL TRUSTEES STUDY THE AGENDA and its extensive background material for several days prior to the meeting. That is the reason they can sometimes vote on important matters with little or no discussion at the board meeting.

THE BOARD TAKES ACTION only on those matters listed on the agenda. Petitions, requests and similar items presented to the board are acted upon at a later meeting, usually the next one.

IF YOU WISH TO ADDRESS THE BOARD. . .

ABOUT AN ITEM please fill out the form below on this page and give it to the Board President before the Meeting starts. When the board gets to this item on the agenda, the board president will invite you to come forward and speak. A five minute limit is imposed unless otherwise waived. The board will take no action at this, but if necessary, the item will be placed on the agenda for a future meeting.

TO THE PRESIDENT

LOCKHART BOARD OF TRUSTEES

I would like to speak to the board concerning the following agenda item:

Subject, if NOT on the agenda:

Name:

Title:

Organization:

Address:

Phone:

[On the back of the leaflet are facts about the schools and staff.]

Figure 7.2. (continued).

become less angry. When the board *really* listens to opinions, they may glean new information that will assist them in modifying policies and procedures.

A regular public forum may be helpful. Larger districts provide for public input by meeting at different campuses. These meetings have a limited agenda and the board makes no decisions; the only purpose is discussion. For example, the Board of Trustees of Tomball, Texas, meets on the first Monday with the staff and community to celebrate educational programs and accomplishments. They meet the following Tuesday for business meetings.

COMMUNICATING IN FRONT OF THE PUBLIC

When the job is one of words, there must be discipline in talking . . . what is talked about, how the talking occurs and when it is done.

Carver (1991), p. 169

At one board training, the novice trustee informed me that role-playing board discussion was unnecessary, because "if the trustee had done their homework, there was no need for discussion." I disagree. Communication *is* the board's work! Each student advocate must be highly skilled in discussion and dialogue. How else can they use their collective wisdom to identify and generate solutions for complex problems?

The challenge of establishing an effective communication system with angry and resistant trustees can seem as overwhelming as forging a raging river. Over and over again, they will encounter conditions that will severely test their resolve. But they must persist in not only establishing an authentic communication system, but continually monitor the system to make sure that it is effective. When the system goes down in times of conflict, find the problem and repair it.

Communication is more complicated during board meetings; on non-routine matters, policymakers must explore complex issues from many points of view. It is difficult to be agreeable, supportive, and knowledgeable while challenging, probing, and questioning assumptions and ideas. To be understood, all must agree on the meaning of important words and avoid educational jargon. As a courtesy for the audience and each other, they should explain the reasons behind statements, questions, and actions.

When the board trustees have taken the time to identify their common values and mission, their communication is more likely to demonstrate honesty and respect. When trustees are unable or unwilling to share their knowledge, perceptions, and ideas, they are signaling their estrangement from each other. As a deliberative body, all must demonstrate supportive, not divisive, communication.

All trustees must participate in important discussions, since without total involvement in the decision-making process, commitment will be weak and implementation of decisions may be sabotaged. Individual differences are honored. Everyone is heard with respect; no one's feelings and opinions are rejected as inappropriate. Even those who are naturally quiet and respond infrequently must speak up, if only to agree with other speakers.

As with any group, if stronger persons take the lead and less assertive ones remain in the background, communication and relationships will remain shallow and guarded, resulting in weak decisions. No one should monopolize the discussion; each must share pertinent information without grandstanding or preaching. To provide context for information is one thing – to fill the air with words is a waste of valuable time.

An essential aspect of effective communication is to lay everything on the table that is pertinent to the conversation. If voting against the majority, tell why! To learn a crucial detail after the decision has been made impairs the effectiveness of the corporate body. Unfortunately, many people share information in the parking lot, on the phone, or in the lounge. Avoid such sabotage and discourage others doing so. Such behaviors stir up energy and fail to determine facts of generate solutions.

When committed to resolution of interpersonal conflicts, trustees speak *directly* to each other about concerns, expectations, and feelings. Board business is discussed as a group, in legally constituted board meetings, not in "meetings after the meetings."

Gathering pertinent information is crucial to success as a member of the board, but few of us know how to ask questions. We prefer to talk. But, if you want to gather information, you must ask questions that will increase your awareness, understanding, and knowledge of activities. Asking clear and important questions is essential in becoming an effective board member.

First decide what information you need and then ask the richest question you could ask in connection with that issue. Questions that can be answered Yes or No reveal little. "Rich" questions are ones that provide a quantity of information. You can judge the question's effectiveness by the quality of the information you obtain.

Here are samples of rich questions:

- What is the problem?
- What do you think we should do?
- What have we tried already?
- What are the consequences?
- Who ought to be involved?
- When will you have an answer (report, more data) for us?
- Is there anything else we should know?

Effective problem solvers must generate lots of answers. When everyone contributes and gives his/her best, alternatives flow. Then assess the dangers and opportunities of each option. Examine each one to see how well it could work out on the one hand and how badly on the other. Ask a lot of *What if?* questions. If the board still cannot make a decision, then you may need to return to the beginning to seek a better question to generate the best decision.

Board meetings must focus on the educational needs of students, instead of bids for milk and school buses. Instead of petty bickering or lengthy discussions regarding building maintenance, board meeting time should be used to collect and discuss information necessary to create a high-performing educational system. When there is trust between the board and superintendent and everyone comes prepared, meetings can be pleasant happenings instead of marathons.

During board meetings, the superintendent serves as a consultant, making recommendations, answering questions, and providing context. Because the board has been kept up-to-date on specific educational programs, they are able to make informed decisions regarding resources, policies, and staff.

EXECUTIVE SESSIONS

The issues discussed in executive sessions, away from public observation, are the really difficult ones. Away from public observation, trustees must make decisions about such moral dilemmas as expelling students:

> Why does the board need to make the decision when they have only the information presented to them. I suppose it's only a formality, but why? Well, only thing I can see is the board gets bad looks when the parents are upset at them for what they've done. But it's really not the board, it's the principal recommending expulsion. It's like we're the jury, but we don't take near enough time to investigate who's telling the truth. It seems like one day some child is going to get a "bum rap."

> Our decision has to be based on what the principal and the superintendent say. But if we aren't going to investigate, then why do we have to vote on it? I've talked to other trustees and they say, "Just do it. It's the way it's done."

> It's the biggest item that has bothered me so far. I don't mind having to expel a student, I just don't think we should have to make the final decision if it's already a done deal. Some student is going to get a bum rap and may decide not to complete school on account of it. Board should have more time. I'm going to bring it up. I'm not going to just rubber stamp everything.

Personnel decisions, legal issues, property decisions, and student expulsions are protected under sunshine laws to protect people's rights and the interests of the district. No votes or decisions can be made in executive session and all discussion must pertain to the stated reason for the executive session.

Because of the strict legal restrictions, trustees must be even more clear and purposeful about their discussion during and after executive sessions. Even though out of the public eye, each participant should continue to demonstrate courtesy and respect to others. A true and correct record of the proceedings is maintained. The entire board should then decide what is to remain behind closed doors, what should be communicated to the public, and by whom.

STAMP OUT MICRO-MANAGEMENT

> Moving mountains an inch often appears less active than moving mole hills a mile. Boards who would be strategic leaders must move at a more deliberate pace than their staff, but with issues far more momentous.
>
> Carver (1991), p. 194

The most common complaint about boards by superintendents is their delight in micro-management. Such micro-management leads to less effective school organization (Chubb and Moe, 1990). From my research and experience, micro-management is caused by the agenda, the superintendents, the trustees, and the legislatures.

Superintendents contribute to micro-management by providing agendas full of trivia. One superintendent told me that he could have the board minutes available for an 8:00 A.M. staff meeting the morning after the board met *since he completed the minutes at the same time he created the agenda!* In other words, the board's work is a formality. No surprises expected!

When I ask trustees why they meet so often, the usual response is: "We're in a building mode. We're meeting with architects/contractors/building superintendents." In such cases, trustees have become superstaff! Highly trained and qualified persons are being minutely scrutinized by a diverse group of amateurs!

Boards collude in the efforts to waste their time on trivial issues, perhaps because they have not determined their primary task and responsibilities. "To the hammer, the whole world is a nail." Trustees may perceive their responsibility as an extension of their business expertise. The lawyer perceives everything as a legal issue. To former educators, supporting the teachers may be their primary goal. Instead of providing for an effective counseling and guidance program for *all* the district's children, an individual trustee was pleased with scholarships and college information she had provided for selected students on her own. The trustee who is a building contractor gets personally involved with building contracts.

With the best of intentions, trustees become micro-managers, not a governing board. It is easy to understand why a plumber would feel more comfortable checking the pipes in the new school than setting policies and approving staff to carry out such work. But time on the trivial eliminates time and energy for policy issues and creates a leaky accountability system. How can you grade the cook if you contributed to the soup?

Self-imposed micro-management will be eliminated when the governing body understands the power of policies and trusts the superintendent and staff (and their own decisions!). Because they have approved the personnel policies, salary schedules, guidelines for hiring and non-renewal, and evaluation procedures, they assure the most competent staff is creating a high-performance learning program. The board confirms that staff recruitment, selection, and development are consistent with district goals. Details regarding placement, promotion, attendance, expulsion, suspension, graduation, conduct, discipline, safety, health services, food services, and transportation services are left to the staff.

When the corporate body has hired a qualified building contractor, the board will not oversee bids, contracts, and progress, but inspect and approve the product. Updates should be included as information items in the board packet or disseminated in a weekly (or bi-weekly) update.

When a trustee becomes aware that the agenda-makers are overloading the agenda with minutiae, it is prudent to visit with the board president and the superintendent. Trustees should not allow anyone to intentionally waste the board's time; it makes them look foolish. If trustees are deliberating on inconsequential issues to avoid dealing with a more difficult one, the board president or other trustee should bring the discussion back to the more serious issue.

State legislatures can move boards out of micro-management by eliminating their own micro-management. "Each state should examine its body of law to free school boards from excessive regulation while revising accountability methodologies" (Walker, 1992, p. 7).

BOARD SELF-EVALUATION

Meeting Evaluation

(*1*) Was the agenda well prepared, focusing on strategic (mostly educational) issues?   Yes____ No____

(*2*) Does the agenda focus on the educational program?
                                           Yes____ No____

(*3*) Is the board packet available to all members at least four days prior to the meeting?   Yes____ No____

(*4*) Does every trustee read the board packet and ask for further information as necessary?   Yes____ No____

(*5*) Is relevant, non-confidential information from the board packet available for the audience and press?
                                           Yes____ No____

(*6*) Does the board president create and maintain a pleasant and collaborative atmosphere, with all trustees actively participating?   Yes____ No____

(*7*) Is every board meeting conducted in accordance with state law and regulations?   Yes____ No____

(*8*) Is the public welcome at all meetings and invited to participate following board-adopted policy?   Yes____ No____

(*9*) Did the board follow their policy on audience participation?
                                           Yes____ No____

(*10*) Do the trustees follow agreed-upon rules of order?

Yes_____ No_____

(*11*) Do all trustees participate during the business portion of the meeting?

Yes_____ No_____

(*12*) Do trustees communicate clearly, directly, and to the point?

Yes_____ No_____

(*13*) Do trustees press their views without really listening to any other suggestions?

Yes_____ No_____

(*14*) Do trustees rush to find a solution to the problem/question instead of being clear about what the real problem/question may be? Yes_____ No_____

(*15*) Do trustees get bogged down by internal politics and let board meetings become a forum for power play?

Yes_____ No_____

(*16*) Do trustees go along with the majority view, failing to express an opposite opinion? Yes_____ No_____

(*17*) Do trustees admire decisions for their speed rather than wisdom? Yes_____ No_____

(*18*) Are executive sessions held only as necessary and conducted in accordance with state law? Yes_____ No_____

(*19*) Does the superintendent serve as a consultant to the board, providing professional expertise and advice when requested?

Yes_____ No_____

(*20*) When a decision has been reached, does each trustee support the decision? Yes_____ No_____

(*21*) Did conflict arise? Yes_____ No_____
How was it handled?

(*22*) Does the board keep to their time commitments?

Yes_____ No_____

CHAPTER 8

Governance Tools

ALTHOUGH many people believe that boards will always stumble from rubber stamping to meddling and back again, I believe it is because they do not understand the true power of the governance tools available to them. Effective boards collaborate with the community to create the vision for the educational system and implement that vision when they select a wise superintendent, create policies, and build the budget on district goals. Because they have built a solid foundation, they are able to evaluate the success of the educational leadership, policies, and budget. They understand that these powerful governance tools ensure accountability by stating expectations and goals.

CREATING THE VISION

> One of the most powerful ways of achieving change is to imagine in vivid detail a desirable and achievable future and then build a part of that future in the present.
>
> Arthur Waskow

It is the local school board's responsibility to determine the district's vision, mission, and goals, provide human and financial resources to implement its goals, then evaluate success. The planning process assumes that all stakeholders will be represented; consensus is the norm; and the outcome will be worth the effort, time, and resources. Without a doubt, such collaboration takes more time than one (or a few) individual(s) acting alone, but long-range planning is most successful when all the stakeholders of our educational program are involved in exploring the future; without full participation and buy-in, the results are subject to sabotage.

The board should create, review, or adopt a mission statement that establishes the unique purpose for which the organization exists and the specific function it performs. It should describe, not the means, but the ends, or purpose of the organization. It should be simple, easily understood, and remembered and incorporated in any planning documents. As community members, parents, staff, and students create a common language, they develop motivation and commitment to implement the vision. Here is a sample:

> The mission of our district is to provide a learning environment that prepares our students for success in an ever-changing world.

Such a community-based activity enables the superintendent, board, and community to determine barriers and support for each student's success. During this process, the community becomes a supporter of continuous educational improvement, and all are knowledgeable about educational trends, student needs, and the barriers to educational success. The leadership team then use the goals to determine the policies, programs, and resources necessary to implement the vision.

SAMPLE OF A GOAL-SETTING PROCESS

(*1*) Step I: Establishing the framework, parameters, and anticipated outcomes:
- What are our common values?
- What do we want our students to know and be able to do?
- Select the planning process.
- Determine roles and responsibilities. The superintendent will

- initiate and oversee process
- recommend facilitator
- provide staff, resources, and information as needed
- establish communication process between facilitator, staff, board, and community
- provide for implementation and evaluation
- The board will
  - provide focus, resources, support, direction, and parameters for planning process
  - adapt, approve proposal and processes
  - establish goals and parameters
  - determine oversight committee selection process
  - approve all plans
  - define own goals based on the results
  - establish superintendent's goals based on district goals
- Define success: what will success look like?

(2) Step II: Scanning the environment
- Where are we now?: baseline data
  - campus, district, state goals
  - academic test results
  - new and emerging programs
  - demographic information and trends

(3) Step III: Determine strengths, weaknesses, opportunities, and barriers
- input from community representatives
- input from educational staff

(4) Step IV: Advisory committee creates report

(5) Step V: Board receives report and selects three to five priority areas

(6) Step VI: Staff creates action plan

(7) Step VII: Board approves action plan

(8) Step VIII: Staff implements plan

(9) Step IX: Board and staff monitor results

(10) Step X: Evaluate and modify

Neither the board nor individual trustees get involved in the *im-*

plementation of the goals. It is the superintendent's job to opera-tionalize the goals with the support of the staff and community. The board tells *what ought to be,* then evaluates *what is!*

THE POWER OF POLICIES

Although the board's power lies in its role as policymaker, I have yet to meet a board that appreciated the power of policies. When boards understand how policies achieve the results they want, I believe they will attend more carefully to their develop-ment, review, and use and behave much differently from one that sees itself as super-staff. "By attending directly to policies, the governing bodies address that which has enduring importance: vision and inspiration" (Carver, 1991, p. 29).

The essential continuity of purpose, vision, and structure for educational excellence depends on the board's ability to maintain a steady course despite changes in superintendent and board membership. Policies ensure such stability in programs and or-ganizational structure and move the board from a reactive to a pro-active stance by setting parameters and direction. The policy manual is the "bible" of governance.

A policy represents a course of action that is deliberately adopted after a review of possible alternatives. Although staff or citizens may initiate requests for policy development or review, generally policies are recommended for the board's consideration by the superintendent. They may be based on federal and state laws, court decisions, or local needs. In order to ensure that poli-cies and regulations are not in conflict with applicable law, they are usually reviewed by the district attorney prior to adoption by the board.

These policies are broad guidelines prescribing the organiza-tion and program of a school system. They create a framework for the governance of the district by establishing oversight proce-dures, standards of accountability, and adequate planning for future needs. They set in place a definite course of action or a pro-cess to guide present and future actions.

Comprehensive policies improve the efficiency and effectiveness of the educational program. When policies describe the roles and responsibilities of the leadership team, relationships improve. They enhance efficiency by enabling the superintendent and his or her staff to discharge their assigned duties with continuity and consistency, since administrators will not need to make decisions regarding the myriad of details that occur daily. There is too much to decide, too great a variety of situations for each person to consider each situation as if nothing like it had ever appeared before. Policies ensure that when people operate, even under pressure, they can act with a consistent pattern.

Policies also ensure support and visibility of educational programs. With the move toward site-based decision making, policies are even more important, as they ensure districtwide continuity of programs and provide parameters for campus decisions. They provide an outline of the program, giving it emphasis and direction. When incorporated into policy, programs, procedures, and practices are institutionalized so that a program does not disappear when its director leaves the position.

Policies secure the board's position so that, when under fire, they have a secure footing. For example, when the board has adopted an effective policy regarding the selection, adoption, and review of instructional materials, they encourage the resolution of parent concerns *before* a public crisis looms. When these student advocates have adopted a student discipline plan, they can expect all student handbooks and staff behaviors to support and implement that plan. Because they have approved the budget and receive regular updates, they can approve expenditures on a consent agenda; only major discrepancies need attention.

With well-written policies *that are followed equitably,* many personal conflicts can be avoided. Making policies available to the public may avoid ill will. When the policy regarding public participation at board meetings is available to citizens, for example, they will know why they cannot have a conversation during meetings with the trustees, and that items not on the agenda cannot be discussed at board meetings. When parents or other members of the community are concerned about textbooks, provide them with the policy describing the citizen review process.

Unfortunately, boards often adopt policies without considering the interactive effect of new policies on older ones. A policy that emphasizes success for all students, for example, may need to review and revise its policies on student discipline, student handbooks, alternative educational settings, staff evaluation, etc.

Because policies clarify expectations, they provide for accountability. The board should receive periodic reports on programs and activities to ensure that its adopted policies are followed. Because it has built measurable outcomes into the policy, it can evaluate the outcomes and determine if the program or procedure is successful and if not, why not.

However, the best policies in the country are of no use if they are unknown and unread. Trustees must have access to the board policy manual and refer to it often. The table of contents enables the board to determine omissions that need to be remedied. If the policy manual is too cumbersome, consider providing sets of key policies for each trustee. Each trustee must have a copy of the board's roles and legal responsibilities, the district's mission and goals, grievance procedures, and communication with the community. Your board may select others that will keep them focused on educational issues and out of the courtroom.

THE BUDGET

The district budget is often the largest of the community, but the lay members of school boards have little knowledge of budgets, tax rates, bond issues, etc.

The budget: that's been the most difficult thing so far. When I came on in August they had already gone over it. I needed to vote and approve it. I hever realized how much money the school district deals with and where all of it goes. And, uh, I'm not a real good mathematical person so I have to be able to trust those people doing the budget. And I know the man who does the budget, I've known him, I've lived in N all my life . . . I've known him forever and I know he's good, so I could basically trust him and agree with what was in front of me. Now that I look back I wonder if I should have asked because I didn't know enough. Not that I would have thrown it out and made them start all over, but just a few things here and there.

MR: There's things you voted on, approved, but now you're thinking, why did I do that?

We had to vote on the budget as a whole . . . it is thick . . . can't tell you how many items. Later, well maybe I should have asked about it.

MR: What would you do differently?

Girls' soccer team, need for more counselors, wonder about putting money toward counselors rather than the girls' soccer team. Maybe that could have been put off a little bit longer.

Next year? I'll be prepared. Actually knowing the people that I'm working with better. I know them because I was raised here, but working with them is a different thing. Talk with board members a lot more. Go through the budget piece by piece. I had to vote on the finished house without seeing the blueprint. They had budget workshops, but I didn't have prior history about budget workshops.

Allocating resources during times of shrinking budgets requires complex decision-making skills. What factors should be taken into account? What are the options? What questions must be asked? How do you set priorities? How will community values influence the decisions? How will you provide assurances to the community that you have met the needs of the students economically?

All boards would benefit from an activity provided to the students of Dr. Nolan Estes, former Superintendent of Schools in Dallas, Texas. He passed out copies of a school district's budget and a sheet of paper with twenty questions. The students were to find the answers to all the questions, using the prepared (and approved) budget.

The students found that seeking the answers generated new questions. Finding out how much was spent on "personnel" depended on *where* in the budget we looked, since there were several "personnel" entries. We wondered why the athletic and music budgets were separated from the rest of the budget.

But it was the last question that confounded us all. "Does this budget meet the needs of the students of the school district?" Many students (like many boards?) answered "Yes! The income matches the total budgeted amount."

I fussed and fumed. "I don't know anything about the needs of the students of this district! Are the results of a needs assessment here somewhere? Were there public presentations? Is there a graph showing the relative amounts spent in the various categories? How can we answer the question? We haven't the necessary background information!"

That, of course, was exactly the point! Without background information, a needs assessment and agreed-upon goals, how can you justify the budget? It is essential that board workshops and public forums regarding the budget be well publicized. All citizens need to understand the larger context of school funding and feel confident that their money is being spent wisely; those on fixed incomes justifiably fear tax hikes.

When the public is part of the decision-making process, they will have a better understanding of the challenges of providing a strong educational program within budget limitations. When they attend budget hearings, they learn about population trends, faculty-student ratios, and the expense of special programs. Community members who have been involved with the long-range plan, staff, parents, and students should be able to explain the interrelationship of the budget with the educational program. Because the budget is based on and aligned with the district's long-range plan, they will be able to justify innovative programs, additional technology, and staff development.

Because resources will always be scarce, trustees must work within financial limitations to secure the best facilities, maintenance, and staff. Cutbacks at both the state and national level have caused creative solutions throughout the country. Some districts have allowed advertisements on school buses, gyms, sports teams' jackets, newsletters, maps, district reports, and stadium walls. A district in Oregon is growing a cash crop for a grass producer. Many districts have a full-time grant writer who generates his/her own salary as well as funds for innovative programs.

Here are some possibilities to cut district costs:

- Encourage students to graduate in three years. If you spend $5,000.00/year per student, early graduates save that amount. (The most recent Texas legislation guarantees a $1,000.00 scholarship at a state college for three-year graduates, still saving about $4,000.00 for the early graduates.)
- Have an energy audit conducted for all buildings. There are now professionals to develop a program to save many times their fees in utility savings.
- Survey other maintenance and operations expenses. Our schools are indeed filling up and falling down. Decide if the cheaper choice now will cost more later. Delaying maintenance costs may add expense long-range.
- Share services with neighboring districts or local social service agencies. When the library, playground, and buildings are used by the entire community, those larger political entities can provide some of the financial support.
- Physical and mental health services, drug use prevention, parenting, and safety programs should be provided in a "seamless delivery system" by the community. Such collaboration also reminds the community of their responsibility for the mental and physical health and well-being of their younger citizens.
- Consider a plan to encourage your more experienced (and better paid) teachers to seek early retirement. (But beware of losing too many experienced mentors at once!)
- Consider the cost/benefit ratio of athletics and vocational education. Could some of those costs be supported by a school/business partnership?
- Consider privatizing services to save direct costs and provide more efficient services.

Members of your community and the educational staff are able to generate other useful ideas to save money. Ask them!

The board must agree on their vision and mission before they can feel confident about approving the budget, since there are values and priorities imbedded in the final product. Even with 80 percent or so encumbered by staff salaries, decisions are made regarding which staff and which programs. The budget must reflect the results of the planning process.

Another useful suggestion from Dr. Estes is that when a windfall occurs after the budget has been created (let's say $100,000.00), instead of spreading it throughout the budget, put it in one place, say gifted education, where it will have a noticeable impact.

Before you approve the budget, be sure you know the answers to these questions before the public asks them of you:

- Is the budget based on/aligned with the district's strategic plan?
- What staff reductions or additions are incorporated in the budget?
- Why is the proposed budget increase greater than the rate of inflation?
- How will local property taxes be affected by this budget?
- How much revenue will the district receive from state sources? Federal? Other sources?
- Is there funding set aside for possible district growth and additional staff during the year?
- What programs or services have been reduced or enlarged this year? Why?
- What percentage of the budget is spent on instruction? What percentage on athletics? Electives? Other optional programs?
- How much does our district spend on the special education program?
- What proportion of the budget consists of mandated costs? Discretionary?
- What percentage of the entire budget do we spend on administrative costs?
- How do we compare with other districts of our size?
- What strategies have been used to eliminate waste and improve efficiency?

- Are we providing adequately for maintenance of our facilities?
- Is there a long-range plan for capital improvements? What are our anticipated needs?
- What percentage of the budget will be spent on staff development?
- And the most important question of all: Does this budget meet the needs of our students?

EVALUATION AND ACCOUNTABILITY

Accountability is the condition of being accountable, liable, or responsible. It is a participatory process to determine what persons can and should do, about the resources and conditions needed to do them, and then whether they have done them. The basic idea is that school systems and schools or, more precisely, the professional educators who operate them, should be held responsible for educational outcomes—for what children learn. Curriculum, teaching-learning strategies, and services must be evaluated to determine if they are meeting the needs of their intended recipients. We must not continue to fund efforts that are not productive.

The emphasis on evaluation of school systems and their programs is a result of the growing tendency to look at educational enterprises in terms of cost effectiveness. It also provides a way to make school systems more directly responsive to their clientele and communities. The debate over accountability is bound to help us think more precisely about our goals, how they can be achieved, and how we can reassure ourselves about the degree to which they have been achieved.

It is the board's job to request information, such as financial status, information regarding the physical plant, student assessment data, and reports on programs and personnel. It asks questions to elicit the necessary information, such as: Is the physical plant being maintained to ensure the ability of the staff to carry forward the educational program? Do staff need an expanded professional development program to ensure success for all students?

Should resources be shifted to support weaker programs? Then it can compare results and progress toward its established goals.

This monitoring process is the backward look that assures the board that the ship is sailing smoothly toward its destination. The board is provided information based on agreed-upon criteria and focused on specifics, remembering always that *students* and *student achievement* are the focus of attention. During this process, the board is able to evaluate its own policies and procedures, adjusting and adapting its work accordingly.

Because the board has clarified the expectations and limitations of the superintendent and staff, all evaluation methods are based on data and reports that describe successes and failures in achieving such goals.

SETTING GOALS FOR THE BOARD

Workshop Agenda

[This agenda is indicative of custom-designed workshops created for a single leadership team. Each agenda is modified prior to the workshop, based on assessed needs and critical incidents at the time of the training event.]

Objectives

At the conclusion of the workshop, the board will

- Create/update their district's mission statement.
- Create tools to evaluate and monitor the superintendent's performance.
- Evaluate and monitor their own performance.
- Develop an action plan to improve performance.
- Review current policies regarding their goals.
- Develop and prepare an implementation plan.
- Establish accountability.
- Evaluate educational outcomes based on measurable criteria.

Establishing the Foundation

- Review the policies regarding board and superintendent responsibilities regarding district planning.
- Review the mission statement.
- Use tools to evaluate our progress.

Building on the Foundation, Moving toward the Future

- district planning process
- the goal setting process
- needs assessment: challenges and opportunities for our district
- reviewing current policies
- developing the plan
- implementing the plan
- establishing accountability
- evaluation procedures

Workshop Strategies

- lecturettes
- small group work
- large and small group discussion
- review of selected literature
- evaluation of pertinent policies

BOARD SELF-EVALUATION

Creating the Vision

(1) Have we involved the entire community in setting our long- and short-range goals?   Yes____ No____

(2) Do we use our mission statement as a foundation for our board meeting agendas, budget, and policies?

Yes____ No____

Policy Development

(*3*) Is the board's policy manual available to trustees, staff, and the public?   Yes_____ No_____

(*4*) Does the board create, adopt, review, and follow policies that ensure effective and efficient governance?
     Yes_____ No_____

(*5*) Does the board review and update its policies on a regular basis?   Yes_____ No_____

(*6*) Do we review policies before adoption to determine their congruence with existing policies?   Yes_____ No_____

Fiscal Responsibility

(*7*) Does the budget reflect the district's long-range or strategic plan?   Yes_____ No_____

(*8*) What strategies have we considered to eliminate waste and improve efficiency?

(*9*) Are facilities being adequately maintained?
     Yes_____ No_____

(*10*) Has the board adopted a long-range plan for capital improvements and budgeted for anticipated needs?
     Yes_____ No_____

(*11*) Does the budget support professional development for all?
     Yes_____ No_____

(*12*) Does the budget reflect equity and excellence?
     Yes_____ No_____

CHAPTER 9

Managing the
Socio-Political Challenges

When the placid world of governance, like the usually dry arroyos of the Southwest, becomes a flash flood, rains surge through these channels altering the features of the educational community.

Wirt and Kirst (1982), p. 99

UNCLEAR EXPECTATIONS OF EDUCATION

ALTHOUGH Americans invented mass education, we argue continuously about it and what it is for. Who do we educate and to what ends? How do we meet the dual challenge of meeting world competition and fulfilling society's felt needs? The many stakeholders in our educational system are constituents with diverse goals and expectations.

Business and industry continuously increase their expectations of our graduates and urge schools to align themselves more closely with the needs of the workplace. Government reports assume that students are not being adequately educated and encourage national assessments for all students. Content specialists encourage educators to restore a core curriculum and encourage curriculum audits and alignments. Conservative political groups influence the adoption of textbooks and the ability of schools to address social issues such as teenage pregnancy and AIDS.

123

REPRESENTING THE COMMUNITY

Public education's attempts to deal with these contradictory expectations have created a unique environment, full of contradictions. Who does the individual trustee represent? Newly elected members of a school board may feel obligated to the specific constituency that elected them. They are likely to allocate resources or make decisions biased in favor of their constituents: the parent-teacher group, the teachers' association, the business community, the retired community, or a specific neighborhood.

However, as citizens participate on the school board, they become more sensitized to the importance of providing financial support to the educational system. They are more reassured about the quality of teachers, the curriculum, and school discipline. As they increase their knowledge of the educational community, they move away from the views of their constituents until it is difficult to predict the position a trustee will take simply by knowing the preferences of constituents in that district (Sergiovanni et al., 1987).

Trustees must know the values of their own community, but unless they develop a process to continually ascertain the community's values and opinions, they will not be aware of concerns. Although some states attempt to provide for better minority representation by creating single-member districts, it is a continual challenge to represent the increasingly diverse constituencies.

When the community's values or composition has shifted and a politically active constituency seeks a stronger voice in school governance, they will elect a trustee with dissimilar goals and values from the incumbent's. Serious disruption of the governance process results, including, often, the exit of the superintendent (Lutz and Merz, 1992; Spring, 1988). Political pressures subject both superintendents and trustees to high turnover, leaving staff and students with confusing messages, fluctuating goals, and "this year's new thing."

NATIONALLY FUNDED PRESSURE GROUPS

Turbulence has resulted in many communities when a growing

number of people narrow their vision of education to their own religious, social, economic, or other personal values. Competing ideologies regarding the content and process of education have affected school governance as boards have become embroiled in controversies and expensive legal battles over graduation prayers, textbook selection and removal, sex education, and guidance programs. Whether a "holy war," "guerrilla warfare," or a "shotgun wedding," this ideological battle between educators and the New Christian Right has created a renewed public involvement in education and election of school trustees.

Religious groups have built coalitions to influence school governance through the election of trustees and a focus on parental rights, safe schools, a basics curriculum, and school choice (Reed, 1993). Mr. Simonds, of the Citizens for Excellence in Education (CEE), tells school administrators that the agenda of CEE is to return academic excellence, moral sanity, and family values to schools and elect parents to school boards who will hire parent-sensitive superintendents (Simonds, 1993). Although the nominal targets include outcomes-based education, self-esteem programs, health education, and prayer in schools, the larger issue is "how future generations are to behave and what America is to be. Education is their paramount preoccupation" (Kaplan, 1994, p. K-1).

Some of the criticisms may be the result of misunderstanding educational terminology and buzzwords. Educators and trustees must involve more community members in the decision-making process, so that goals and aims will be shared. The entire community benefits when interest overcomes apathy and knowledge overcomes ignorance.

SCARCE AND UNCERTAIN FUNDING

Facing constituents about budget decisions is a source of continual frustration for all boards.

> When a group is in an environment of scarcity,
> it frames its experience in terms of survival.
>
> Smith and Berg (1987), p. 188

The realization that many school children have inequitable opportunities for an excellent education has created a demand for excellence and equity. Students from deprived educational and socio-economic environments must be afforded first-rate educational services. Legislatures and judicial requirements mandate greater services yet provide no funding. Resources to meet these demands are short; fiscal crisis is the norm, leaving the local boards trying to do more with less. Implementing extensive and expensive mandates limits the board's ability to carry out its district's goals. The resulting frustration distracts from educational issues.

Districts need a secure and adequate financial base to provide an adequate budget. The funding process should recognize a multitude of needs and supply the dollars to meet those needs. Devising a plan that re-allocates dollars to provide equity, but places a cap on excellence is not a solution. To provide individualized instruction and a computer to every child is not financially feasible.

In addition to the challenges of doing more with less, many boards are frustrated with the *uncertainty* of funding. Legislators often fail to provide numbers to districts until long after they need to secure teacher salaries and contracts. Funding formulas vary leaving districts unable to create a budget until well after the school year has begun. After agonizing over one financial cap all summer, boards are sometimes told they will receive even less money. Do they break contracts with teachers? Stop payment on textbooks? Disallow any staff development? There are no easy decisions! The board has pared to the bone, all that is left is the marrow!

LEGAL AND JUDICIAL REQUIREMENTS

Novice trustees are amazed at the legal constraints on their role. Legal requirements delineate duties and responsibilities and constrain board meetings. School law regulates budgets, taxes, contracts, and corporate ownership of property. Due process, fair elections, nepotism, and provisions for students and staff with special needs are legal (and financial) issues.

There are legal obligations regarding records, conflicts of interest, libel and slander, qualifications of trustees, and election laws. Local policy must fulfill legal mandates regarding special education, environmental issues, and relationships with employee organizations. Students are protected under admission, attendance, discipline, and expulsion regulations. Both students and staff are protected under non-discrimination laws regarding race, gender, sexual harassment, and disabilities. Personnel law covers employment, evaluation, and dismissal of personnel. The superintendent's appraisal and evaluation process also has legal aspects.

Requirements and constraints are so pervasive that the number of firms specializing in "school law" is expanding at an exponential rate. Actually, most of the current content of board training could be covered under a "School Board and the Law" heading! (It has been my experience that the best current board training is provided by members of the legal profession.)

EDUCATING TODAY'S STUDENTS

After an intensive day of board orientation, the moment of truth arrived.

"OK," said the trustee, "what's wrong with American education, anyway?"

"Well," I replied, "there are many answers to that question; let me tell you a story that may help."

> I have a friend who is a single parent. We were making plans to meet for breakfast the next Saturday morning. "Will you have your son that weekend?" I asked. "I don't know," he said. "Sometimes I don't know until late, then I go over to his mom's and carry him back."
>
> "You mean," I asked, "that when he goes to sleep he doesn't know where he'll wake up?"
>
> "That's true," he said. "But he doesn't seem to mind."

Try to imagine going to sleep and never knowing where you will wake up! In addition, the mother is moving out of state soon and the parents had not yet determined who would keep the child. The father was "afraid" it might be him.

I paused for a few moments for the trustees to imagine this kindergarten boy's life, then I continued.

This child is the most anxious four-year-old I know, yet neither parent is aware that children need security to be emotionally healthy. Instead of the healthy laughter of most children, when *he* plays, his shrieks are heard all over the apartment complex. Such lack of stability is not uncommon, causing students to be anxious and restless in class. Teachers must create stability and security for these children so students can learn in the few hours of the school day.

The trustees just stared at me. They had no idea, yet most educators have dozens of such stories!

With limited funds, local school districts are attempting to provide for the educational needs of an increasingly diverse body of students. We are educating more students from low socioeconomic and troubled backgrounds and nontraditional families. At the same time that demands increase, the constituency that has a direct stake in education has diminished; the number of families with children has declined to less than 30 percent. These demographic changes are having a powerful impact on the ability of school boards to meet the diverse educational and economic expectations of multiple constituencies.

More and more, the students who are going to populate our schools will be precisely those students who have historically been least well served there. The most important current problem facing educators is the inability of our instructional programs to adapt successfully to the educational needs of children who are not achieving or otherwise not being fulfilled in these programs as they are operating today.

Sergiovanni (1994)

Trustees must learn about the psycho-social needs of children in their district that are barriers to learning. What services are provided for abused and neglected children? Many students have individual challenges, such as learning and or physical disabilities, and represent diverse backgrounds and cultures. Poor students and children from troubled backgrounds and nontraditional families often share a sense of alienation, low sense of efficacy, and demand for instant gratification. We can learn to cherish the diversity of our students, but it creates an incredible tension as we try to respond to all the differences children bring as they cross the yard and come into the school.

Educating these children requires more resources, staff, technology, and training. Teachers need longer hours, smaller classes, and stress management because of the intense demands of these very needy children. When boards are aware of the societal factors and community pressures affecting educational progress, they make appropriate decisions regarding social and educational needs of students. They assure the community that all staff are well-trained and child-centered.

FUTURE-ORIENTED EDUCATION

> Do not re-create the schools of your youth. They must be relevant for today's students working in tomorrow's world!
>
> Daggett (1993)

The rapidly shifting nature of our economy will require greater skills, knowledge, and expertise than ever before from each individual. These new skill requirements, combined with changing demographics, will force new approaches to how and what students learn, the organizational patterns of our schools, and the roles of educators, parents, and communities. Our nation's future productivity is linked to the full participation of each individual; *all* students must be prepared to meet the challenges ahead, not just a few.

Unfortunately, we don't even know all the challenges. Many of today's jobs won't exist in the year 2000. Tomorrow's economy will require an even better-trained workforce — one in which workers will have to be taught new skills several times during their working lives. Workers must be lifelong learners, performing new tasks effectively in unpredictable and rapidly changing situations. Re-engineering and improved technology make many jobs more complex. Functions previously performed by several different persons are combined into one. Even entry-level jobs require collaboration, problem solving, and a high level of communication and interpersonal skills.

The growing technological complexity of the workplace demands technologically literate graduates and expensive educational services. In 2010 the right of all school children to have access to technology in all its forms will be as important as their right to textbooks is today (Worth, 1995).

Effective leadership requires that we provide the best possible learning environment for all our students within the available resources. We must determine not only *where we're going,* but *how we are going to get there* — the *journey,* as well as the *destination.*

BOARD SELF-EVALUATION

Discussion Questions

(*1*) What are the board's primary responsibilities?

(*2*) Who are *my* constituents?

(*3*) Who are *our* constituents?

(*4*) How do we determine our community's values and opinions?

(*5*) Do we involve community members in our program committees?

(*6*) What special needs do our students have and how do we provide for their education?

(*7*) What student support system do we provide for our students?

(*8*) How do we provide for career guidance?

(*9*) How do we provide for effective communication between administration-teachers-students-parents-community?

(*10*) What process do we have to continually improve our curriculum?

(*11*) How do we determine curriculum content for future needs?

(*12*) Do we provide technology for all students?

CHAPTER 10

Becoming an Advocate for Educational Innovation

> Tomorrow's economy will require an even better-trained work-
> force – one in which workers will have to be taught new skills
> several times during their working lives.
>
> Mead (1995), p. 42

WHILE the ever-changing workplace requires greater skills, knowledge, and expertise than ever before from each graduate, economic, social, and personal factors cause many of our children to attend school poorly-equipped emotionally, physically, and/or socially. These conflicting forces require new approaches to organizing schools so that all students can be successful. In today's global economic market, each district's graduates compete for jobs and education not with each other, but with graduates from around the world.

School boards are at risk precisely because they have not been sufficiently vigilant in guaranteeing children a high-quality education, but, too often, local school boards are unaware of their role in educational reform. In order to generate understanding and support for success for all their district's children, trustees must know the psycho-social barriers to learning and innovative methods used by successful districts.

To gain perspective about current issues, concerns, and possibilities for your district you must be familiar with the underlying assumptions and expectations of public education. *What are schools for?* Who are the students and what are they doing there?

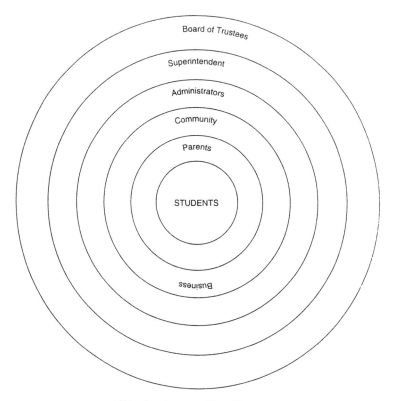

Students are the Focus

What are they *learning* here? What are the underlying assumptions and responsibilities of this public institution? In order to provide the best possible learning environment for all students within the available resources, you must know what is wanted, what is needed, and what is already happening in your district.

DETERMINING NEEDS

In order to be a change agent you must know where you are as well as where you're going. You might begin with the "two by four by six" model of schooling (two covers of a book, four walls of the classroom and six periods a day). The two covers of a book represent the curriculum or the content. The four walls represent the physical structure(s), and the six periods a day represent the order, sequence, and timing of schooling. Although it is a limited view of schooling, the "two by four by six" curriculum is still as evident in today's schools as it was one hundred years ago. We must be conscious of its limitations.

If your board is typical, you have acquired only fragmented information about the content (the curriculum) and quality of instruction. Do you know the content, materials, and success of your district programs? How are media and technology used? What do you know about the physical setting for students and employees? Is time fluid or static in your district? Is there flexible scheduling? Extended day? Extended year? How does your district compare with the best educational programs and strategies? Do you know how prepared your graduates are for college or the next phase of their life?

As a parent, community leader, and citizen you have already learned a great deal about what's happening in school. You have heard stories from your children and others'; staff and neighbors have called, and you've read newspaper articles and test results. Bear in mind that, although all information is useful, some sources are more reliable than others. Because of the importance and magnitude of decisions you must make as a school trustee, supplement anecdotes with a foundation of accurate information. As you increase your own knowledge and awareness, work with others to put all the pieces together to create a composite portrait of your district. Only then will you be able to make informed decisions.

To provide perspective and context, consider the information using these basic categories: Why? Who? What? How? How Well? When? and Where? Use this general information as a framework to organize information about your district.

WHY ARE WE HERE?

The mission statement defines the reason the board and the district exist. It is usually created during a long-range planning process. When developed by community members, parents, staff, and students and adopted by the board, it becomes a reality check and assessment tool for the educational program. The board uses the mission statement and long-range goals as a focus when it makes decisions regarding the budget, curriculum, staff, and the educational environment.

WHO WORKS HERE?

Most of this information is required by state and/or federal regulations and is reported often, so it should be easy to acquire such information from the superintendent. You won't need to remember all the details, but you probably will wish to have a snapshot of all the persons involved in the educational process in your district.

Who are the students in your district? What ages attend schools in your community? What kind of early-childhood program is available? Is there an adult and/or a continuing education program? What about special needs students? What is the profile of the students by gender, socio-economic status (SES), and ethnic categories?

What about the staff? Who are they and what do they do? Novice trustees are surprised to learn the numbers and talents of the staff involved in the educational process. Bus drivers, custodians, coaches, counselors, social workers, principals, volunteer coordinator, architect, and building contractor enable the educational process to run smoothly. Any or all of them are affected by the board's policy and budget decisions and should be included in the district improvement processes.

WHAT DO STUDENTS LEARN IN YOUR DISTRICT?

Even more important, who decides what students learn and how they learn it? No matter the mode or method, the *formal content* of what students learn is called the *curriculum*. It may be driven by mandated tests, state-adopted textbooks, and/or media. It may have been created locally by staff or purchased.

What is the *scope* (the extent and content of what is learned) of the curriculum? What is the sequence, in what order is it taught? Most districts also pay attention to how the curriculum is *aligned.* For example, is the fifth grade curriculum built on information learned in pre-kindergarten through fourth grade? Just as teachers of Algebra II must know their students have learned the concepts of Algebra I, teachers must know what students have learned prior to attending their classes. This "alignment" attempts to assure that concepts are included at the appropriate place in the curriculum.

HOW ARE STUDENTS LEARNING?

Strategies for teaching and learning are often determined by the personal style of the teacher and/or current popular strategies. What strategies are in use on your campuses? How is technology incorporated into the teaching, learning, and organizational aspects of the district? Are teachers using multiple strategies for many learning styles? Student- and teacher-led discussions? Lecture? Worksheets with only one correct answer for each question? Do students work cooperatively or alone in silence? Are the staff using cooperative, experiential, and mastery learning?

HOW WELL ARE THEY LEARNING?

As a trustee, it is your responsibility to monitor student learning. That is your *evaluation* role. Again, some information is required by state and/or federal regulations, but you will probably receive additional information from the superintendent.

Results of state-mandated competency exams or nationally normed test data inform you more about students' ability to repeat isolated facts than their thinking skills. Even so, comparing results over time and noting disparities between sub-populations of students is useful. The term disaggregated data is used to describe the results of separating information by categories.

This separated data tells you more than clustered totals. For example, your district may have high test scores, but if those high-performing students are predominantly in one ethnic group, the staff needs to determine why the disparity exists and seek ways to remedy it. Which campuses are doing well? Why? Historically, low socioeconomic-status (SES) students have done less well in school, but many schools have found ways to accelerate their instruction so they can be successful.

The superintendent will also share information regarding numbers or percentages of students in special programs, and numbers and kinds of prizes, scholarships, and awards. You also need to know the extent and kind of discipline problems and strategies for managing them. Student-teacher ratios are helpful in determining if programs are adequately staffed. Numbers of students over-age for grade and students who fail to complete the academic program are another way to discuss the successes and failures of the current program. What strategies and programs are in place to remedy disparities and promote student success?

WHEN DO THEY LEARN?

What hours of the day and night? What days of the week? What months of the year? Students are learners every waking moment and only a small portion of what children learn is within the school setting. They were learning long before they ever showed up at the schoolhouse door and they continue to learn in ways beyond our grasp and control.

Our students learn on the information highway and from the ever-expanding world of multimedia, their family's behavior and communication patterns, and, certainly, their peers. Suburban youth spend hours every weekend at the mall, urban youth on the streets, and rural and small town youth in various outdoor settings. How does your educational program connect with their worlds?

WHERE IS LEARNING TAKING PLACE?

Classrooms, campuses, playgrounds, fields, tracks, community centers, and/or nurseries are all appropriate educational environments. Today's students learn in chemistry and computer labs, on track, baseball, soccer, and football fields, in kitchens and workshops and traditional classrooms with desks bolted to the floor. Some are fortunate enough to learn in hospitals, police stations, hotels, bakeries, offices, strip malls, and bowling alleys, allowing interaction between school and the real world.

Because, "what is learned in high school or for that matter, anywhere at all, depends far less on what is taught than on what one actually experiences in the place" (Edgar Z. Friedenberg), the learning environment of your district is as important as the teaching and learning strategies currently being used. What is the quality of the learning environment for your students? Schools spend a good share of their energies attempting to mold children into a pattern. Are there attempts to encourage conformity like desks in straight rows? Or are students allowed to be energetic, creative, and spontaneous?

Consider three kinds of relationships on that campus: the way teachers relate to students, the way teachers relate to each other, and the way administrators relate to reachers. Do you find evidence of cooperation, collegiality, respect for the student's personality and mind?

Using Sergiovanni's criteria, what evidence do you find that this is

- a caring community?
- a learning community?
- a collegial community?
- an inclusive community?
- an inquiring community?

PHYSICAL PLANT

As a parent and interested citizen, you are no stranger to your child(ren)'s campus(es). You have visited some campuses for special events, such as parent-teacher meetings and dramatic or musical programs. In addition, the superintendent has provided opportunities for you to tour all district buildings as part of your district orientation.

Use your campus visits to sense the overall quality of the learning community as well as the physical plant. Is this a place you would willingly spend time? By using all your senses you will quickly learn that each campus has its own feel, climate, atmosphere. Be aware of this atmosphere and energy of the building. As you walk down the halls, listen for the pitch, volume, and quality of speech. Are teachers shouting to gain control or is everyone speaking respectfully to each other? Communities of learning are busy and purposeful but not necessarily quiet. Intercommunication between all the learners (adults and students) may be a quiet hum, or a cacophony of sounds.

Determine whether there is adequate and effective maintenance. Is the campus overcrowded? Do the buildings smell musty or aromatic? Is space used efficiently? Are all buildings inviting and painted and furnished attractively? Although learning can be messy, the rooms should be cleaned often.

Ask to visit the teachers' lounge. Is it messy and filled with cast-off furniture or decorated with care? Professionals deserve attractive working conditions. Providing an attractive place for planning and renewal helps teachers to feel valued and appreciated.

When you join your child for lunch, how does the cafeteria look, sound, smell, and feel? In addition to the quality of food, is the space too small and crowded? A too-quiet cafeteria should cause as much concern as a noisy one. Children may be forbidden to speak to each other because of a time crunch. When will they learn communication skills, if not during meals?

One elementary school had a class eating on the stage of the cafetorium. The tables had cloths and there were "curtains" simulating a real restaurant. This class was being honored for behavior or academics (I don't remember which!) in an inexpensive, but highly visible way. Whenever I needed to visit with the principal, I could locate him in the cafeteria, visiting with the students. Can you tell, even without ever visiting the school, how pleasant it is to be on that campus?

Standing in a school hallway when the bell rings is always an interesting experience. Are the students respectful of each other's space? Are they considerate of slower moving students? Is the language positive or rude? Are there too many bodies for the space leading to tardiness and tension? In the best schools, high school hallways are pleasant even when the bell rings; students move confidently to their lockers and classrooms with teachers conspicuously monitoring the proceedings. Students (or teachers!) loitering in the halls after the bell rings could be cause for concern.

THE WIDER WORLD OF EDUCATION

The concern of many current and former superintendents (including the ones running the state and national conferences) is that specific information may increase trustees' propensity for micro-management. That is understandable. Remember, your role as a trustee is not to operate or interfere with the educational program, but to use information to make wise decisions that support the educational program. You will be able to govern more effectively when you are aware of the broader academic context.

To gain awareness of current issues, concerns, and possibilities for your district and around the state and country, you must become more familiar with the larger context of education. For the broader context of education beyond your district, there are many publications and conferences. A visit to your school's professional library or the library of a nearby campus will provide a world of information. Every professional group has an association, an executive director, publications, and conferences at the state and national level. All are excellent sources of information.

For example, in 1995 a hot topic of discussion in many journals and associations was "inclusion." You may be more familiar with the term "mainstreaming," which was required by P.L. 94-142, requiring all students to be educated in the least restrictive environment for their needs. Students were taken out of special education classes and mainstreamed for at least a portion of the day with the hope that, eventually, they would be in regular classes.

Lately, however, advocates for special needs children are urging that most, if not all, children should be educated in the regular classroom: included. So the term *inclusion* has become a word that represents a host of meanings and viewpoints. By comparing several publications for those in special education as well as for parents and teachers of gifted children, you will get a sense of one of the many timely issues. By now, another issue will be "hot," but the necessity of comparing viewpoints will always be valid.

PREVENTING FADDISM IN THE DISTRICT

> We trained hard . . . but it seemed that everytime we were begin-
> ning to form up into teams we would be re-organized. I was to
> learn later in life that we tend to meet any new situation by re-
> organizing: and a wonderful method it can be for creating the illu-
> sion of progress while producing confusion, inefficiency and de-
> moralization.
>
>   Petronius Arbiter, 210 B.C.

Maintaining a balance between the status quo and continual innovation is difficult but essential. Educators must discriminate among a plethora of educational tools, strategies, materials, and possibilities. Sometimes programs are adopted and implemented without good (any?) research. Experienced teachers have grown weary of fads that come and go with every new principal or superintendent.

Because the board of governors is expected to advocate for innovation while satisfying the constituency, it falls on them to "preserve order amid change and to preserve change amid order" (Alfred North Whitehead). The board must ask: "What works and how do we know?" As elected representatives, trustees must consider the educational priorities for their community, its families, and all students.

The board must plan for continuity amidst the chaos of change. They must insist that students acquire a sense of belonging through scheduling and organizational arrangements that provide for communities of learning. There must be an alignment between the curriculum and the nature of our children, based on the community's values and the anticipated outcomes of the learning process. The curriculum should demonstrate respect for the diverse backgrounds and capacities of students.

Fashionable new programs frequently have little bearing upon real problems or unique needs of the district or campus. One of the anticipated advantages of school-site management is to overcome this shortcoming, as each campus selects programs and strategies to meet the challenges of its unique student population.

Here are some questions trustees might ask about a new program a superintendent has introduced to the board.

- What need/problem/concern is being addressed by this program? Is this need currently being addressed in other ways? If so, how successful is the current program?
- Why is this change/innovation/strategy being recommended? What is the problem we are trying to solve? What are the anticipated results?
- What does research tell us about this program's effectiveness with students such as ours?
- What is the implementation plan? (How will we implement this program?) Who will be responsible for implementation?
- Will we pilot this program before we implement it districtwide?
- Is it congruent with our mission statement and goals?
- Is it consistent with our local policy? Strategic plan?
- What is the cost? in time? in $$$? (What is the source of the funding?) in personnel?
- What staff development will be required? How will that be done?

If the superintendent is not forthcoming with acceptable answers, further research may be necessary and the topic should be tabled until answers are available and acceptable.

Although research from many sources has provided a plethora of information about school reform, most innovations are never fully implemented because they are not fully supported. We know that new programs and strategies need leadership from an administrator or group of teachers. Teachers are more likely to support (not sabotage) the innovation if they believe it will benefit their students and they have the necessary time, materials, and other resources. Staff need support from internal or external consultants and, sometimes, additional training.

The challenge for most of us is to not wax nostalgic about our own schools, but to determine a curriculum that will be relevant for today's students working in tomorrow's world. In addition to reading, graduates must be able to read and write technical manuals. Not only basic arithmetic, but they must be familiar with complex math, including statistics, logic, probability, and measurement systems. In addition to biology and chemistry, they need applied physics. Social skills are also important: students must learn to cooperate, communicate, and problem-solve. Above all, they must *learn how to learn,* since workers will be taught new skills several times during their working lives for jobs that don't even exist yet.

A NEW MODEL OF EDUCATION

> Boards must create the conditions of invention in school systems; they must ensure that . . . leadership is provided by those they employ to serve the interest of the community and its children.
>
> Schlechty (1990), p. 12

We must imagine the achievable future for education and work continually to ensure its success. Research has shown that the organizations of academically successful schools and academically unsuccessful ones are rather different. The former tend to have goals that are more focused and ambitious, to be headed by purposeful educational leaders, and to be staffed by teachers who work with one another and with the principal as a community of professionals—as a close-knit team. Unsuccessful schools tend to hold lower and more ambiguous expectations of their students, to be managed rather than led, and to be staffed by teachers who are lacking in the requisites of professionalism and effective interaction (Chubb and Moe, 1990).

Educators must talk not about what is taught but what is learned. Using research and knowledge gleaned from cognitive psychology, we acknowledge that learning is an active and participatory affair, so we create opportunities for understanding, using dialogue, real-world experiences, and opportunities for full engagement. The students' own sense of purpose and efficacy is the principal stimulus for learning; their ideas become the foundation. We take what students already know and think about as a point of departure for new learning. We expand the basics to include the related background and foreground so that students learn *in context*.

Here are some examples from a school where students are taught for understanding:

- Fifth graders experiment with pendulums and refine contrasting hunches about timing and length into testable theories.
- The history class learns that history is not only a record of facts, but also the complex moral and political enterprise of reinterpreting the past.
- Geometry students build computer models of alternative solutions to problems.
- All students use writing to understand themselves and the world.
- All students are valued and expected to learn to the best of their ability.
- There is a sense of mission and commitment of all to that mission!
- All buildings are safe, well-maintained, inviting, and furnished attractively (including the teachers' lounge!).
- Much of the learning is in small groups and collaborative.
- Students are grouped into nongraded teams.
- Student-teacher relationships are long-term.
- Each campus has a positive school climate and is a caring educational community.
- Personal planning, goal setting, and career awareness are integrated into the curriculum.
- Curricula and learning processes are adapted and modified to meet the learning needs of each student.

- Academic decisions are based on assessment data and students' learning styles.
- Cultural diversity is celebrated!
- There are only positive communication patterns between and among adults and students; everyone expresses himself or herself effectively and appropriately.
- Students value their time in school and use their time well.
- There is a low truancy, tardy, and dropout rate.
- Discipline is fair and consistent, with a focus on prevention.
- Everyone takes responsibility for his or her own behaviors; all demonstrate appropriate social skills.
- Students are acquiring the cognitive, affective, and behavioral skills necessary to function successfully now and in the future.
- Each campus is a community of learners and workers.
- There is ongoing professional development for the entire staff, based on assessed needs.
- Problem solving, decision-making, and planning skills are demonstrated.
- Everyone demonstrates respect for self and others.
- A continuous and comprehensive guidance program supports emotional, social, educational, and career development for all students.
- Educators and the community work together to share human resources, learning opportunities, mentors, health, and community services.
- Persons who are addicted or who have ongoing psychological needs are receiving services from the appropriate mental health providers (within or without the system).
- A wellness orientation is demonstrated: appropriate diet and regular exercise are valued; everyone practices self-care.
- Everyone's artistic, musical, and other creative talents are nourished!
- Technology is available for all.

BOARD SELF-EVALUATION

Providing Leadership for Educational Improvement

(*1*) Has the board adopted a strategic plan and approved an implementation plan?   Yes____ No____

(*2*) Do all trustees understand the district's mission and support other members of the leadership team in carrying out that mission?   Yes____ No____

(*3*) Does the board allocate resources based on the district's educational goals?   Yes____ No____

(*4*) Does the superintendent share information relating to educational trends, topics, and programs on a regular basis?
                                                      Yes____ No____

(*5*) Does the board ensure that a quality educational program is available to all the district's students?   Yes____ No____

(*6*) Has the board determined the *kinds of knowledge* to be shared in the local school system?   Yes____ No____

(*7*) Do all trustees demonstrate interest in school events by attending frequently?   Yes____ No____

(*8*) What conditions has the board created for sustaining a leadership system that will, over time, drive the school district toward excellence?

(*9*) In what way does the board provide leadership that serves the interest of the community and its children?

CHAPTER 11

Growing a Better Board

IMPROVING THE GOVERNANCE MODEL

> Until school officials and policymakers learn to base their deci-
> sions on the realities of life in the classroom—on the issues that
> confront teachers and students who make education happen every
> day—education policies and reforms will continue to fail.
>
> Pauly (1991), p. 36

OUR educational systems are faced with twin challenges. On the
one hand, we have children with more and greater needs; on the
other, we have increasing needs from the marketplace. Tomorrow's economy will require an even better-trained workforce. Information is exploding at a fantastic rate; what was true yesterday
is out-of-date tomorrow. Technology is commonplace in most
workplace environments. This often requires different teaching
methodologies and materials than are currently provided.

The resulting economic interdependencies and competition
have created a renewed interest in the public education of tomorrow's workers. Seen as both the problem and the solution, the
educational system is buffeted from all sides. As expectations of
schools become ever more complex, many theorists have re-
visited our model of school governance. Are they to become
policy boards (Carver, 1991; Danforth, 1992)? Are they to provide
stability and support within change (Schlechty, 1990)? Are they to
represent their constituency or become trustees *separate* from the

people that elected them (Lutz and Merz, 1992)? Will they become brokers of the new lay forces in school affairs (IEL, 1992)? Are they to select and support a superintendent, then simply sanction administrative actions, as many superintendents prefer? Or will they become extinct?

> I think that the days of the volunteer board have long since passed. It is time for school districts to be run as the businesses that they are. Professional educators, not part time volunteers, are what the patrons and kids need in control.
>
> Matt Graves, personal communication

LINKING SOCIAL AND EDUCATIONAL NEEDS

> The number one priority is support services. There is nothing wrong with the schoolhouse. Teaching has advanced to a state of the art that is unparalleled in mankind. The difficulty is putting the kind of support into those schools that will make a difference. We need aid for needy children, no-parents children, drug-addicted children, raped children.
>
> Raymond (1989), p. 1

When boards are aware of the societal factors and community pressures affecting educational progress, they make appropriate decisions regarding social and educational needs of students.

As Sarason (1990) reminds us, just as "the medical community does not accept responsibility for cancers caused by smoking, pollution, food additives and scores of other possible carcinogens, the educational community cannot accept responsibility for problems originating in the larger society. Not that educators will not deal with them or that educators will not try to seek better approaches, but that these problems will be intractable as long as they are seen as the primary responsibility of educators" (p. 38).

The Danforth Foundation has provided a model for schools and social service agencies to work together to serve students more effectively. It urges local school boards to become a powerful force for reform, creativity, and support for the real needs of children.

Three goals become the core of the redesign of the roles and responsibilities of the local governance body:

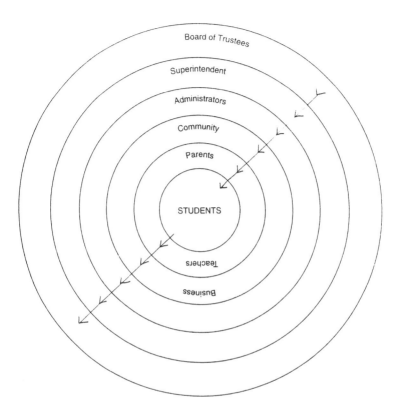

Influences on the Students

- All children should meet world-class educational standards.
- There is accountability for what happens in schools.
- What happens in schools is tied to other services for children.

These policy boards become responsible for setting broad guidelines, establishing oversight procedures, defining standards of accountability, and ensuring adequate planning for future needs. Districts partner with other organizations in a seamless delivery system to integrate education, health, and social services. Funding will follow the students, allowing flexibility in funding to meet special needs.

DETERMINING ENDS AND MEANS

What if we used a more effective framing of the governance challenge that not only eliminated common problems but cleared the way for boards to be strategic leaders? In *Boards That Make a Difference* John Carver (1991) describes his Policy Governance Model®, a redesign of the board's role. School boards that make a difference focus their time and energy on the *ends* of education. They spend their time and energy defining the skills, understandings, and attitudes that public education should bring about for children.

Boards that have embraced this model discriminate between the roles and responsibilities of boards (the ends) and the administration (the means). The board agrees on a small number of policies to define the action and authority parameters for the staff and determines a monitoring system to evaluate performance. It then gives the superintendent authority to achieve the publicly determined results without board interference.

The board creates policies in four major areas:

- ends to be achieved
- means to those ends
- board-staff relationship
- the process of governance itself

GROWING A BETTER BOARD

Some boards have greatly improved their ability to become effective governing bodies as a result of a comprehensive board development program and organizational support. They focus on their role as policymaker and stay out of the micro-management trap. As a corporate body they clarify issues, summarize contributions, propose new ideas and courses of action, give and receive information, and coordinate ideas and suggestions.

Effective boards agree on, communicate, and follow their guiding values. These values are integrated into their critical activities: the development of policies, the setting of goals, and the allocation of resources. They gather information and model effective communication. Using their mission statement and strategic plan as a foundation, they make wise decisions to monitor performance and hold personnel accountable. These local boards of education, as true servant-leaders, provide a quality education for *all* our students.

This book has described many reasons why boards fail to behave as educational leaders and how state legislatures, superintendents, associations, educators, and the community share responsibility for the current system. The incentive to improve governance will come from those citizens, legislators, trustees, and educators who understand the importance of effective school governance.

Legislators must bite the bullet and fund all mandates! Funds must be allocated equitably and in a timely manner so boards are not continually revisiting the budget, instead of attending to educational matters.

They must rescind state-mandated micro-management. There is little incentive for school boards to be better leaders of public education if their opportunity for leadership is constantly eroded. The legislature should be encouraged to examine its body of law to free school boards from excessive regulation while revising accountability methodologies. Many governance problems are caused by the voluminous laws and regulations for which boards are ultimately responsible. Micro-managing from the capital causes poorer local governance, not better (Carver, 1991; Walker, 1992).

Eliminating multiple election dates would help to overcome voter overload and apathy. One election date for trustees of the local school board and community college and city council members could increase voter turnout as well as reducing costs.

Citizens must overcome their apathy and vote! If the voters are not concerned for their children, they are probably concerned about taxes. The community should provide for excellent publicity, public forums, and convenient election dates. To encourage quality citizens to become candidates, the media should promote and elect candidates who have the capacity, integrity, and wisdom to perform well in this high-pressure position.

The community must support the leadership team in identifying problems and needs of the district. Boards should never have to justify their need to improve their leadership skills through board development programs. The media should represent meetings fairly so that all will understand the legal and judicial constraints on board operations. Information about the role enables everyone to be realistic and fair with his/her demands and refrain from projecting unrealistic expectations and demands on the position.

Business and industry must encourage capable employees who are interested in the role to become trustees, then provide time and resources for them to serve well. Because interpersonal and leadership skills are needed by all, they could open their many executive training programs to educators and school trustees.

Candidates for the local board must decide, before election, whether they have the time, energy, and capacity for educational governance. Before they file, they should attend board meetings until the very end of the meeting, not just the public forum! They must be willing to bring about desired changes through legal and ethical processes, *as a board,* not as individuals. Making promises on the campaign trail may make good headlines but demonstrates poor statesmanship.

In order to support educational reform, govern effectively, and perform competently, candidates must understand the political, socio-economic, and demographic context of their role. If such information is not forthcoming from the local district, the candidate should seek it from incumbents or the state school board association.

Elected trustees must restructure the role and change their behavior. As members of a board, they must decide whether they want to steer the ship or rearrange the deck chairs. In order to govern effectively, they must overcome the forces impeding their ability to carry out their role. They can refuse to collude with those that wish to divide and conquer. They must allow no barriers to interfere with the governance of successful schools.

They can demonstrate respect for one another and the superintendent at all times. They understand their role is not matrix management, but they must speak with one voice. Board meetings become a dialogue about things that matter. They refuse to be distracted by inconsequential details and maintain their focus on the educational needs of the district's students.

They must use their time and energies to carry out the district's strategic plan and goals. They base their decisions on a community-created mission statement and long- and short-range educational goals. These goals then become powerful tools to evaluate the success of policies, curriculum, and staff. They ensure that leadership is provided by those they employ to serve the interest of the community and its children (Schlechty, 1990).

And of course, they display ethical behavior at all times!

The *superintendent* must work with the *board president* to provide for ongoing board development from orientation to standard operating procedures and educational programs. They must create agendas congruent with educational goals and the best use of the collective wisdom of the trustees. They use consent agendas when possible for routine matters. They respect the time and energy of the board.

As the operation of educational institutions continually becomes more complex, the skillful leadership and teamwork of the board and the superintendent are essential. The board and superintendent must become a *leadership team,* developing and maintaining harmonious interpersonal and group relations while adapting to community pressures. They must clarify the difference between administration and governance to avoid conflicts.

The team should identify the problems and educational needs of the community, achieve a working consensus on priorities, agree on strategies to implement them, and collaborate effectively on the required actions. This team creates the vision for the district and becomes advocates for the best possible education for their students.

Professors of educational leadership should provide information and skills for our educational leaders to thrive in the political context of educational governance. To keep their boards well-trained, superintendents must know how to educate adults, manage groups, and create the conditions for effective meetings. Professors and superintendent associations could provide information to enable superintendents to use the collective wisdom of elected community leaders as partners in school improvement.

National and state board associations should provide thorough research and technical assistance for all their members. They should identify key issues for local boards and provide resources to manage them. They should provide relevant and powerful conferences of the same quality provided for executives. Because effective governance requires knowledge of the interdependence of good governance and systemic school reform, boards should have current information about educational restructuring within the state, national, and international context.

Although states vary in the specifics of school governance, all board presidents must have access to a comprehensive board development curriculum that improves school governance. They must describe the role accurately with all its responsibilities, complexities, constraints, and challenges so there are fewer surprises for new trustees. The associations should ascertain characteristics of effective governing bodies, then build high-quality, in-depth board development programs on that foundation.

Trustees must know how social issues, politics, current trends, and issues in education impact their policy-making role. Conferences should include information that enlarges the context of education and provides a higher view of educational governance. They would benefit from presentations by experts in the future, change management, systemic reform, learning organizations, and team leadership. Boards must be kept up-to-date on the world of technology and its impact on learning.

All members of the nation's 6,000 boards of education should be learning advocacy and political skills within an ethical framework to bring the needs of children and education to the forefront of our nation's political agenda.

Board development facilitators must tell it like it is—accurately describing the complexities of education and school governance. Because effective statesmanship requires both content knowledge and process skills, facilitators must provide training that will transfer to the board room. Empowered trustees will then ask clarifying questions, seek and assess information, select and retain those superintendents that are effective educational leaders, and become powerful advocates for children.

To create governing bodies of excellence we must begin today with a new attitude toward board selection, development, and accountability. All stakeholders must collaborate to change the structure of trustee elections, improve the orientation of novice policymakers, and demand better relationships between superintendents and their boards. We must provide information, skills, and support so trustees can form competent communities, then hold them accountable for allocating resources, setting policies, and supporting leadership that ensures success for all our children.

When boards are knowledgeable and informed, skillful and resourceful, interdependent and pro-active, they use their collective wisdom to establish "conditions for designing and sustaining a leadership system that will, over time, drive the school district toward excellence" (Schlechty, 1990, p. 12).

AASA (1993). *Professional Standards for the Superintendency.* Arlington, VA: Author.

Bamberger, R., ed. (1991). *Developing Leaders for Restructuring Schools: New Habits of Mind and Heart.* National LEADership Network.

Bateson, G. (1972). *Steps to an Ecology of Mind.* NY: Ballantine Books.

Batten, J. (1989). *Tough-Minded Leadership.* NY: American Management Association.

Belasco, J. A. (1991). *Teaching the Elephant to Dance: The Manager's Guide to Empowering Change.* New York, NY: Crown.

Belbin, R. M. (1981). *Management Teams: Why They Succeed or Fail.* NY: Harper and Row.

Bennis, W. (1990). *Why Leaders Can't Lead: The Unconscious Conspiracy Continues.* San Francisco, CA: Jossey-Bass.

Blumberg, A. and P. Blumberg. (1985). *The School Superintendent: Living with Conflict.* NY: Teachers College Press.

Brickell, H. and R. Paul. (1988). *Time for Curriculum.* Alexandria, VA: The National School Board Association.

Burns, J. M. (1978). *Leadership.* NY: HarperCollins.

Canada, B. O. (1989). Losing positions. Unpublished doctoral dissertation. Austin, TX: The University of Texas at Austin.

Carver, J. (1991). *Boards That Make a Difference: A New Design for Leadership in Nonprofit and Public Organizations.* San Francisco, CA: Jossey-Bass.

Cell, E. (1984). *Learning to Learn from Experience.* Albany, NY: State University of New York Press.

Chubb, J. E. and T. M. Moe. (1990). *Politics, Markets & America's Schools.* The Brookings Institution.

Cistone, P. J. (1975). *Understanding School Boards.* Lexington, MA: D.C. Heath & Co., pp. 19–33.

Cistone, P. J. (Spring, 1977). Socialization of school board members. *Educational Administration Quarterly.*

157

Conway, J. K. (1994). *True North: A Memoir.* Alfred A. Knopf. NY.

Cottrell, L. S. (1976). The competent community. In Kaplan, B. H., Wilson, R. N. and Leighton, A. L. pp. 195–209 in *Further Explorations in Social Psychiatry.* NY: Basic Books, Inc.

Daggett, B. (1993) The Commissioner's Midwinter Conference on Education: Austin, TX.

Danforth Foundation. (1992). *Report of the Twentieth Century Fund Task Force on School Governance.* The Twentieth Century Fund Press. NY.

Danzberger, J. P., M. W. Kirst and M. D. Usdan. (1992). *Governing Public Schools: New Times, New Requirements.* Institute of Educational Leadership. Washington, DC.

Duke, D. (1987). *School Leadership and Instructional Improvement,* NY: Random House.

Fox, W. M. (1990). *Effective Group Problem Solving.* SF, CA: Jossey-Bass.

Freeman, J. L., K. E. Underwood and J. C. Fortune. (1991). What do boards value? *American School Board Journal,* 1, 32–36, 39.

Friedenberg, J. quoted in E. F. Murphy. (1981). *2715 One-Line Quotations for Speakers, Writers and Raconteurs.* Bonanza Books: NY.

Gibboney, R. A. (1991). The killing field of reform. *Kappan.* Phi Delta Kappa, 682–688.

Greenleaf, R. (1977). *Servant Leadership.* NY: Paulist Press.

Gross, N. (1958). *Who Runs Our Schools?* NY: John Wiley & Sons.

Gross, N., W. S. Mason and A. W. McEachern. (1958). *Explorations in Role Analysis: Studies of the Superintendency Role.* NY: John Wiley & Sons.

Hackman, J. R. (1973). Group influences on individuals. In M. D. Dunnette (ed.), *Handbook of Industrial and Organizational Psychology.* Chicago: Rand-McNally.

Halberstam, D. (1969). *The Best and the Brightest.* NY: Random House.

Harvey, J. (Summer 1974). The Abilene paradox. *Organizational Dynamics,* 64–83.

Harvey, T. and B. Drolet. (1994). *Building Teams, Building People: Expanding the Fifth Resource.* Lancaster, PA: Technomic Publishing Co.

Heller, M. and E. T. Rancic. (1993). Why can't board members act more like board members? *School Administrator,* 40 and 41, 9, 50.

Hersey, J. (1960). *The Child Buyer.* Bantam Books: New York, NY.

Houle, C. O. (1960). *The Effective Board.* NY: Association Press.

Houle, C. O. (1989). *Governing Boards.* San Francisco: Jossey Bass.

Houston, P. (October 1994). A Lens on Leadership; *School Board Journal,* 181, 32–34.

Institute of Educational Leadership. (1986). *School Boards: Strengthening Grassroots Leadership.* Washington, DC: Author.

Janis, I. (1972). *Victims of Groupthink.* Boston, MA: Houghton-Mifflin.

Kanter, R. M. (1989). *When Giants Learn to Dance: Mastering the Challenges of Strategy, Management, and Careers in the 1990s.* NY: Simon & Schuster.

Kanter, R. M. (1985). *Changemasters.* NY: Simon & Schuster.

Kaplan, G. R. (1994). Kappan Special Report—Shotgun Wedding: Notes on Public Education's Encounter with the New Christian Right. *Kappan,* 75:K1–K12.

Kidder, T. (1989). *Among Schoolchildren.* Boston: Houghton Mifflin Co.

Kirst, M. (1989). Who should control our schools? *Texas Lone Star,* 7(5):13–25.

Konnert, M. W. and J. J. Augenstein. (1990). *The Superintendency in the Nineties: What Superintendents and Board Members Need to Know.* Lancaster, PA: Technomic Publishing Co., Inc.

Kozol, J. (1991). *Savage Inequalities: Children in America's Schools.* NY: Crown Publishers, Inc.

Lutz, F. W. and C. Merz. (1982). *The Politics of School/Community Relations.* NY: Teachers College Press.

McNamara, R. S. (1995). *In Retrospect: The Tragedy and Lessons of Vietnam.* NY: Times Books.

Mead, W. (1995). Wal-Mart Government, *Worth:* March, 1995; pp. 42–44.

Morgan, G. (1988). *Riding the Waves of Change: Developing Managerial Competencies for a Turbulent World.* San Francisco, CA: Jossey-Bass.

National School Boards Association. (1987). *American School Boards: The Positive Power.* Alexandria, VA: Author.

Pauly, E. (May 1, 1991). "Classrooms matter more than policies." *Education Week,* p. 36.

Ravitch, D. and C. Finn. (1987). *What Do Our 17-Year-Olds Know?* NY: Harper & Row.

Raymond, J., Superintendent. (1989). *Houston Post,* Sept. 29, p. 1.

Raywid, M. A., C. A. Tesconi and D. P. Warren. (1984). *Pride and Promise: Schools of Excellence for All the People.* American Educational Studies Association.

Robinson, G. E. and P. M. Bickers. (1990). *Evaluation of Superintendents and School Boards.* Arlington, VA: Educational Research Service.

Rosenberger, M. (December 1994). Challenges to Effective Boardsmanship, *Executive Educator,* VA: American Association of School Administrators.

Rosenberger, M. (Summer, 1995). The Administrator's Role in Team Development. *Journal,* Texas Elementary Principal's Association.

Rosenberger, M. (Winter 1993). The Role Acquisition Process of a School Board Member in Texas. *Journal of Texas Public Education.* Texas Association of School Boards.

Rosenberger, M. (Jan/Feb 1993). Joining the Team. *Texas Lone Star.* Texas Association of School Boards.

Sarason, S. B. (1990). *The Predictable Failure of Educational Reform.* San Francisco, CA: Jossey-Bass.

Schlechty, P. C. (1990). *Schools for the 21st Century: Leadership Imperatives or Educational Reform.* San Francisco, CA: Jossey-Bass.

Senge, P. M. (1990). *The Fifth Discipline: The Art & Practice of the Learning Organization.* NY: Doubleday.

Sergiovanni, T. J. (1994). *Building Community in Schools.* San Francisco, CA: Jossey-Bass.

Sergiovanni, T. J., M. Burlingame, F. S. Coombs and P. W. Thurston, 2nd ed. (1987). *Educational Governance and Administration.* Englewood Cliffs, NJ: Prentice Hall.

Sergiovanni, T. J. and J. H. Moree (Eds.). (1989). *Schooling for Tomorrow: Directing Reforms to Issues That Count.* Boston: Allyn & Bacon.

Smith, K. K. and D. N. Berg. (1987). *Paradoxes of Group Life.* San Francisco, CA: Jossey-Bass.

Spring, J. (1988). *Conflict of Interests: The Politics of American Education.* NY: Longman.

Terry, R. (1993). *Authentic Leadership: Courage in Action.* San Francisco, CA: Jossey-Bass.

U.S. Department of Labor. (1991). *What Work Requires of Schools: A SCANS report for America 2000.* Washington, DC: The Secretary's Commission on Achieving Necessary Skills.

Walker, B. (1992). *Texas School Boards in the 21st Century.* Unpublished manuscript. Austin, TX: Texas Association of School Boards.

William T. Grant Commission on Work, Family and Citizenship. (1988). *The Forgotten Half: Non-college Youth in America.* Washington, DC: Author.

Wirt, F. M. and M. W. Kirst. (1982). *Schools in Conflict.* Berkeley, CA: McCutchan Publishing Corp.

Zeigler, L. H., M. K. Jennings and G. W. Peak. (1974). *Governing American Schools: Political Interaction in Local School Districts.* North Scituate, MA: Duxbury Press.

EDUCATIONAL ASSOCIATIONS AND PUBLISHERS

American Vocational Association. 1410 King Street, Alexandria Street, Alexandria, VA 22314.

Educational Leadership. Association for Supervision and Curriculum Development. 1250 N. Pitt Street, Alexandria, VA 22314-1403.

Harvard Educational Review. Harvard University. Gutman Library Suite 349, 6 Appian Way, Cambridge, MA 02138-3752.

Institute for Educational Leadership (IEL). 1001 Connecticut Ave., NW, Suite 301, Washington, DC 20036.

Kappan. Phi Delta Kappa, Inc., 408 N. Union, P.O. Box 789, Bloomington, IN 47402.

National Association of Elementary School Principals. 1615 Duke Street, Alexandria, VA 22314.

National Association of Secondary School Administrators (NASSP), 1904 Association Drive, Reston, VA 22091.

The School Administrator, published by The American Association of School Administrators. AASA, 1801 N. Moore Street, Arlington, VA 22209.

The School Board Journal. National School Boards Association. 1680 Duke Street, Alexandria, VA 22314.

DR. MICHAL ROSENBERGER is an independent consultant, workshop facilitator, speaker, author, and lifelong learner.

Because of frequent moves while parenting her two sons, she has a wide view of the world. She began teaching in Marietta, Ohio, then served the Goose Creek Consolidated Independent School District (Baytown, Texas) for ten years as Elementary Teacher, Elementary Counselor and High School Crisis Counselor, working with at-risk, special education, and gifted students. Her passion for improving the quality of education led her to move to Austin, Texas, in 1986 to acquire a Doctor of Philosophy degree in Curriculum and Instruction at The University of Texas at Austin.

To support her graduate studies she worked in a variety of settings, expanding her knowledge of organizations, families, and leadership. For education agencies and associations, she created and presented workshops and presentations, developed a resource-bank of leadership development opportunities for school administrators, began the state-wide implementation of a comprehensive guidance program, and researched the role acquisition of school trustees. It was in her role as consultant to school boards and superintendents in Texas that she discovered her niche where she could bring together her knowledge of team leadership, school improvement, effective governance, change management, and adult education.

She provides keynote presentations and workshops for business, community groups, educators, and school trustees on students at risk, school restructuring, change management, effective governance, and team leadership.